HOUSE SHARING AND YOUNG ADULTS

House Sharing and Young Adults offers unique insight into the dynamics of successful house sharing among young adults and questions some of the myths fostered by the negative stereotyping of housemates. Illustrated with research from interviews with young adults, it explores co-residence, interpersonal relationships and young people's development.

Beginning with an overview of the concept and history of house sharing among young adults, Clark and Tuffin's volume also examines the reasons for the lack of research into the area up until recently. It explores key questions, including how young adults choose housemates, what makes a desirable housemate, avoiding complications, the psychological advantages of house sharing, how conflict arises and the impact of house sharing on adult development. The authors challenge the stigma of shared domesticity, demonstrating the potential of house sharing to enhance well-being through companionship while acknowledging the potential pitfalls caused by tension in intimate settings.

House Sharing and Young Adults will be essential reading for both undergraduate and postgraduate students of social psychology, developmental psychology, sociology and anthropology, as well as those interested in group dynamics, housing demographics and discrimination.

Vicky Clark is a PhD graduate in psychology from Massey University in Wellington, New Zealand.

Keith Tuffin is an associate professor in the School of Psychology at Massey University in Wellington, New Zealand.

HOUSE SHARING AND YOUNG ADULTS

Examining Successful Dynamics and Negative Stereotypes

Vicky Clark and Keith Tuffin

Routledge
Taylor & Francis Group
LONDON AND NEW YORK

Cover image: © Getty Images

First published 2023
by Routledge
4 Park Square, Milton Park, Abingdon, Oxon OX14 4RN

and by Routledge
605 Third Avenue, New York, NY 10158

Routledge is an imprint of the Taylor & Francis Group, an informa business

British Library Cataloguing-in-Publication Data
A catalogue record for this book is available from the British Library

ISBN: 9780367751852 (hbk)
ISBN: 9780367751869 (pbk)
ISBN: 9781003161370 (ebk)

DOI: 10.4324/9781003161370

Typeset in Bembo
by Apex CoVantage, LLC

CONTENTS

1

INTRODUCTION

The flatting lifestyle

Sharing is particularly prevalent among young adults in the Western world. To the uninitiated, the commonly employed term "flatting" for house sharing in the UK, Australia and New Zealand can be misleading, as the noun "flat" usually refers to several residences or apartments in one building. The concept now incorporates a range of properties from studio flats to detached suburban houses or inner-city residences modified into multiple flats.[1] In the USA, the term "roommate" is employed to describe a fellow resident: we prefer the terms "housemate" or "flatmate" since these suggest that what is shared is a flat, house or apartment while the alternative suggests sharing a room (bedroom) which is rare. The term also reflects a particular lifestyle, frequently associated with a certain stage of life where shared resources are imperative, but there is more to this way of life than merely the driving incentive of economic convenience.

Usually, but not necessarily, house sharers tend to be single, childless, employed and geographically flexible. Flatting typically involves a communal kitchen, bathroom and lounge, with individual bedrooms often out of bounds to other housemates. Rent is split with housework a general responsibility. Household staples such as milk, tea and coffee are usually shared, as are utility expenses, such as electricity and internet. Flatmates may choose independent catering while others opt to prepare and eat meals together with joint food expenses.

For financially precarious young adults with limited incomes, sharing is a pragmatic option as housing devours a considerable portion of their budgets. This demographic applies to those who exit the parental home on socially legitimate grounds, such as to study or for employment. Those who leave home for problem-related reasons, such as addiction, fostering, family disputes or LGBTQ+ reasons, are more likely to become homeless.[2]

DOI: 10.4324/9781003161370-1

There are rising global concerns about the housing difficulties young adults face as incomes fail to keep pace with rent growth. With declining housing affordability worldwide, landlords are maximising profits resulting in escalating rent prices. The problem is exacerbated by housing shortages, especially at the lower end of the market. While housing supply problems have affected all, young people are disproportionately impacted by cost increases and are effectively priced out of buying or renting a house on their own. No abatement of costs is foreseen in the near future.[3]

In addition to lingering economic uncertainty from the 2007–2009 GFC, many young adults have the burden of considerable student debt. Previously common among students, house sharing is now popular with those in their twenties, thirties and beyond. Joint economic and social forces have resulted in lengthier transitions to independent adulthood, with delayed marriage and parenthood, meaning young adults are flatting for longer than previously. Consequently, shared housing has progressed from being a marginal and transitional accommodation option in the housing pathways of young adults to that of much longer tenure.

Sharing has featured consistently in youth housing for some time and is well documented in the UK, Europe, the USA, Australia and New Zealand.[4] Until quite recently, literature on the topic of house sharing among young adults was scarce. In Northern Europe, the research is essentially confined to housing demographers. In the USA, Frances and Calvin Goldscheider examined patterns of leaving the parental home, including shared housing. In Australia, Kirstin Natalier studied the gendered division of labour in shared living and the ambiguous independence of young adults still economically dependent on parents, while Sophie McNamara and John Connell investigated whether shared housing was regarded as "home". In New Zealand, Rebecca Williamson examined routine everyday operations, focusing on the advantages of preparing meals and eating together. The most comprehensive research on the topic was that of sociologists Sue Heath and Elizabeth Cleaver, who investigated the changing patterns of household formation of young adults, including shared households, in England.[5]

There has been a steadily rising increased research interest in shared housing among sociologists and urban, geographic and social policy planners. All research advocates for greater recognition and provision for this previously marginalised way of life. While each has a different focus, all contribute to a greater understanding of the sharing lifestyle. Primarily, the concern of these academics is for young adults at the lower end of the income spectrum, where the precariousness of a roof overhead can lead to homelessness.[6] In contrast, our study deals with young adults from more privileged backgrounds: students with employment prospects or predominantly postgraduates committed to work and career advancement.

Apart from these studies, the literature on flatting largely takes the form of university prospectus advice and practical guides to flatting, such as Annamarie Pluhar's *Sharing housing: A guidebook for finding and keeping good housemates*, Lauren Earl's *Flatters' Survival Guide* and Tanya Sassoon's *Flatmate Survival handbook*.[7] While there are certainly pointers to successful house sharing for those seeking to enjoy the benefits of communal living, this is not the purpose of this book. Our research examines the dynamics of successful sharing among young adults and questions some of the myths fostered by the negative stereotyping of housemates. Significantly, the two latter titles focus on the unfavourable aspects of sharing.

US-based TV shows such as *Friends*, *Big Bang Theory* and *Super Fun Night* depict shared households as sources of fun, companionship and mutual support in coping with the vicissitudes of daily life. They promote the idea that the stereotype of dysfunctional shared living no longer applies. Arguably, these have added to the popularity of the lifestyle. Conversely, social media is saturated with tales of "flatmates from hell", possibly prompted by John Birmingham's "*He died with a falafel in his hand*" in which he depicts sharing with an assortment of questionable housemates, from the criminal and dishonest to drug addicts.[8] Subsequently, the book was successfully adapted into a long-running stage play and a film. The title refers to finding a flatmate dead from overdosing on heroin. Enter "flatmates" or "roommates" into a search engine and the inevitable results focus on the negative. Newspapers and YouTube headlines abound with "The ugly side of flatting" and "flatmates from hell". Whereas prolific negative media accounts curtail any notion that sharing can be functional, the young adults we interviewed were largely positive about their flatting experiences.

Housing is more than a roof overhead; it is of considerable emotional and psychological importance impacting the relationships of those who share the house. Certainly, mental and physical well-being can be compromised by tension in the intimacy of co-residence, resulting in resentment, emotional strain, hostility and anxiety. While things can always go "wrong", there is ample evidence that sharing can also be a positive experience and a socially appealing way of life. Housemates can provide significant psychological benefits, such as an instant social life curtailing social isolation and the development of close, supportive friendships.

Our research participants did provide some distressing accounts of their own but these were atypical:

I had just woken up I came out from my room
and the screams were coming from Brad's room
when I opened the door to look round
to be like is everything alright
he was having the absolute shit kicked out of him
there was blood everywhere
he slept with some chick and the boyfriend found out
anyway Brad tried to make a run for it
it was like a bloodbath and this guy seriously
he was going to kill him. I was shaking
I was like do I call the police
what do I do nobody's here nobody
like there're five people in this place
and not one person is here right now
so I basically had to listen to the screams
and watch Brad get beaten up

The drama described not only highlights how sometimes the unpredictable can happen but also feeds into the perception of sharing as unappealing and perpetuate the idea that shared housing is an undesirable form of accommodation. The lack of research on the topic enables the negative aspects of sharing to predominate. As Sue Heath and colleagues note, by focusing on the tensions and problems of shared living the complete picture is not drawn. Similarly, traditional households are not always idyllic or without interpersonal problems. Heath et al. question why familial living arrangements are not considered problematic whereas non-kin households are.[9] Given the paucity of research on young adult house sharing, our research aimed to contribute to understanding this way of life, including both pros and cons. While increasing numbers of mature adults are opting to house share, the lifestyle is presently most prevalent among younger adults with this cohort the focus of our attention.

Human social interaction and connection lie at the heart of the discipline of social psychology. As social psychologists, we have long been fascinated by the ways in which people get along in groups, the complex dynamics of how things work when people are connected in meaningful activity and the processes involved in working out the best way forward when things don't quite go to plan. While many have experience in shared living, few have sought to take the study of this seriously. Indeed, it is somewhat surprising that the discipline of social psychology has overlooked the topic of shared housing. This means our research represents one of the few contributions of social psychologists to what is currently known about shared housing among young adults.

While our research has been guided by the conventions of academic social psychology, we have written this book with a general audience in mind. Hence we would hope the book will be useful for anyone who shares an interest in the dynamics of young people living together. Additionally, we would hope the book would be of interest to social scientists including sociologists, psychologists, anthropologists and housing demographers. Our research focus on young adults also means that the book will be useful for those interested in human development as many of the participants in our research moved from the family home towards independent living – while at the same time – had their independence linked to the business of sharing with others in the same developmental phase.

Examination of how young adults in shared households accommodate living with non-kin and manage in challenging economic times offers unique and rich insight into their everyday lives. In this regard, Edward Potter notes, "Arguably, one of the most astonishing omissions in psychology for most of the 20th century has been the study of what people do: their interactions in the home and workplace".[10] The sentiment here is one of surprise that resonates with the failure of psychology to study the simple stuff of everyday life. This book seeks to redress this oversight and provide some insight into the interactions that are at the heart of successful shared living. Similarly, Rachael Scicluna has noted that domestic settings are under-researched and under-theorised, particularly alternative families and homes.[11]

The historical emergence of shared housing in the Western world

Communal living is not a modern phenomenon. Indeed, its origins are ancient, global and enduring. Reviewed within a historical context, the present trend towards house sharing is unexceptional. Hunter-gatherers lived communally, as did monks later and feudal vassals in lords' castles. In Medieval times single-family households were uncommon. During the 1800s, a distinction between living with family and friends began to develop and by the second half of the nineteenth century the notion of the family became entrenched. Agricultural work took place close to home, with families providing a vital source of labour. By the early twentieth century, as industrialisation flourished, urbanisation increased: people started leaving home to work in factories and later offices with accessible accommodations close to work sites.[12]

In the USA, historical records indicate high levels of shared living during the 1800s and early 1900s through the common practice of taking in lodgers. According to Bella DePaulo,[13] during the nineteenth century Americans gravitated to cities seeking work. Boarding houses became places where diverse residents could live affordably and socialise with others in shared spaces. Historians estimate that approximately 50% of American residents in the nineteenth century either lived in or ran boarding houses. Landladies, often with the help of servants, provided food and laundry services. This lifestyle fell out of favour through the second half of the twentieth century, both in practice and in social acceptance. Because of overcrowding in many of these boarding houses sharing became stigmatised. During the Great Depression of the 1930s, those seeking to avoid abject poverty moved in with relatives and intergenerational living increased. Taking in boarders was then regarded as a sign of poverty and therefore disreputable: remaining in the parental household was preferable despite many young people again migrating towards the cities in the hope of finding employment. By the mid-twentieth century, suburban life and the nuclear family dominated, with sharing continuing to suffer from negative stereotyping and associations. While nuclear families are communal, they tend to be less intergenerational with a single set of parents and children, rather than older generations cohabiting in the same home.

Sue Heath and Elizabeth Cleaver note that in pre-World Wars English working-class teenagers routinely left the parental home to enter live-in domestic service, agricultural work or apprenticeships. This type of communal living afforded some degree of independence before marriage. For the more affluent remaining in the parental home until the late 1920s was common for men, while women tended to leave home to marry at an earlier age.[14]

Prior to the 1950s, leaving the parental home in British Commonwealth countries was traditionally associated with marriage. One exception to this was when young adults left home for education, in which case they mostly lived in private, chaperoned boarding houses or segregated hostels. For example, nurses (always female) in training served an apprenticeship-style scheme with compulsory living in hostels under the close supervision of a matron. According to nurses who lived through that era, residential living provided an environment of support, trust, friendship and camaraderie, built on time spent together and the sharing of experiences. There were strict curfews until nurses turned 21, whereupon they could go flatting.[15]

Evidence of same-sex flatting dating back to the 1950s was found in *New Zealand Memories*.

> Easy access to the workplace and social life was the beginning of the flatting "lifestyle" that today is an accepted way of life for young single adults. The difference between then and now is that in the 1950s "mixed" flatting was considered a scandal. Young women gathered together in their chosen flats, while down the road there would often be a bachelor pad and a lot of to-ing and fro-ing would take place between the two.[16]

The "sin" of mixed-gender flatting reflected Victorian-styled morals around the close domestic intimacy involved in sharing and the dangers of relationships producing unwanted pregnancies: all of which changed in the early 1960s with the availability of the contraceptive pill. For the first time in human history, women were able to reliably control their fertility. Subsequently, mixed-gender flatting became more common among students and despite strong objections from elders this household mode quickly became the norm for students. In 1967, the newfound liberation afforded by this way of life was celebrated in James K. Baxter's *A Small Ode on Mixed Flatting*. The 130-line poem was written in response to university authorities, who sought to forbid this practice among students.[17]

> *By fencing the young from fornication!*
> *Ah, Dr Williams, I agree*
> *We need more walls at the Varsity;*
> *The students who go double-flatting*
> *With their she-catting and tom-catting*
> *Won't ever get a pass in Latin*

Economies of sharing accommodation among peers have been embedded as a culturally approved exit from the parental household for decades and a key process in becoming an independent adult. In New Zealand, continuing to live with parents beyond the teens has negative connotations suggesting a lack of independence. Yet currently, substantial evidence internationally indicates growing numbers of young adults are returning home to live with their parents for financial reasons. While there are significant differences across countries, the percentage of young individuals who live with their parents has increased over time. This trend was precipitated by the 2008 recession and subsequent increases in house prices. Returning to the parental home both highlights and hides young people's housing problems: living with parents assures a roof overhead but also shrouds the extent of the housing crisis among the relatively well-off.[18]

Sharing as a housing pathway to independent living

Shared housing represents an affordable and convenient option for young people on limited incomes and plays an extensive role in the lives of many. In the UK, sharing is a common feature in early housing careers. Kirsten Natalier notes that this type of household may be marginalised in the academic literature but for many Australians, it has a cultural heritage and iconic status in popular imagination. This is equally true in New Zealand where flatting is a long-established tradition and regarded as a character-building rite of passage for young adults. Repeated editions of the books *Edmonds' food for flatters* and *More food for flatters* are advertised as showing novice flatters how to move out of the family home and still eat in style, without fuss and within a budget.[19] The 1999 New Zealand film, *Scarfies* depicted the freedom from parental confines experienced in student flatting. More recently, the ubiquitous culture of flatting in New Zealand was parodied in the 2014 film, *What we do in the Shadows*, where even vampires purportedly flat together.

Although evident in continental Europe, sharing is not on the same scale as the UK, USA, Australia and New Zealand. This reflects issues of housing supply and sustainable wages, linked to differing welfare regimes, as well as different perspectives on intergenerational support rendering alternatives more feasible. For example, in southern European countries, including Greece, Italy, Spain and Portugal, it is more customary to remain in the parental home. This is due to strong family ties but also low levels of state welfare provision.[20]

Socialist countries such as Sweden, Norway, Finland and Denmark have the highest rates of single-person occupancy in the world, with 40–45% of households having just one resident. In Sweden when youths leave the family home they typically move into a small apartment on their own. Parents register interest in such an apartment on the birth of the child. The apartments are usually located in a complex where there are large numbers of young adults living independently while retaining a high level of sociability. The availability of these apartments is largely due to good planning on the part of politicians, who in the 1960s initiated a large-scale public housing strategy called *the million program*. Sweden saw increased industrialisation following the Second World War and this put pressure on inadequate housing stock. Hence the program sought to construct a million new dwellings. Given that the population of Sweden was then eight million, this was a highly ambitious building program which aimed to provide affordable housing for all.

Between the mid-1960s and the mid-1970s, more than a million new dwellings were completed. While many of these were initially subsidised by the government, these loans were repaid by occupants over a 30-year period. Most of the designs were for families with two adults and two children, however, a good number were also targeted for youth (students) and were studio sized with one bedroom and one bathroom and shared kitchen areas. These student apartments were built in cities with large populations of university students.[21]

Internationally, it is rare for public housing to be so forward-looking with most plans evolving in a more market-driven haphazard manner. This necessitates more sharing, for example, in 2015 a quarter of Americans between the ages of 18 and 34 lived with housemates, up from 23% a decade prior, according to US Census Bureau data. In Australia, The 2021 Rental Affordability Snapshot exposes the increasingly brutal unaffordability of rental properties across the country for the young and single and shows that many renters are worse off than before the COVID-19 pandemic.[22]

In the past, governments offered adequate protection for the economically stressed by providing social welfare and housing. Such benefits today could act as a safety net for the vulnerable. Globally, with restructuring beginning in the 1980s, access to these benefits is becoming increasingly more problematic and complex and this is reflected in the current homelessness crisis. With an over-emphasis on individual agency, welfare systems no longer function as a protective parachute. Shame and judgement are embedded in the system and the neo-liberal ideology of self-reliance prevails. That the family unit is supposed to be relied upon for help is a potent narrative, but intergenerational resources differ dramatically.[23]

Consequently, shared households are currently increasingly common among young adults throughout their twenties, early thirties and even later years. Student-shared accommodation often leaves much to be desired and is frequently substandard and insalubrious. Whereas the image of a can of baked beans and a broken couch pictorially evokes the student-flatting lifestyle, post-student households are more sophisticated.[24] A quick search on the internet provides many articles about guides for the not-so-young seeking flatmates. Older cohort house sharing is depicted in TV comedies, such as *Golden Girls* and *Hot in Cleveland*. The premise of such shows is that the characters live a life of economically viable consumption, socialising, fun and support. The popularising of sharing through these various shows means that limited time is focused on fundamental issues like dealing with domestic chores and conflict. In addition, they still conform to the dominating narratives of men being sexual predators and women being driven by the need to find a long-term mate. Thus, the media reinforces shared housing as a transitional period, a stopgap measure before settling into the traditional valued role of heterosexual coupling.[25]

Most demographers note that census data does not adequately cover shared households among young adults, making comprehensive reliable statistics hard to come by: statistics frequently aggregate all forms of shared housing, making data misleading. Categories are ambiguous and it may mean that these need to be created to recognise particular characteristics, such as precise age group classification. Systematic underestimation and research on communal living may also be due to its supposedly transient nature.[26]

Why are shared living arrangements among young people under-researched?

Those who have studied the domestic lifestyles of young adults have noted the lamentable paucity of research on shared households. The lack of social and cultural acceptance of shared households, which challenge conventional concepts of home, family and intimacy, may account for the curious oversight of research on the topic. Sherry Ahrentzen[27] maintains that shared housing is regarded as an inappropriate and unacceptable way of life by researchers and policy makers: the lifestyle contradicts the American dream of single-family households, reinforcing the stigma associated with sharing. The supposed benefits of security, order and prosperity are aligned against the purported uncertainty, crime and poverty associated with shared residential living. The single-family house ideal is beneficial to real estate agents, builders, public officials, homeowners and predatory banks and therefore remains entrenched since sharing produces less profit. This is exemplified in New Zealand by the undeniably partisan bank advertisement promoting home loans for disgruntled middle-aged house sharers. The advertisement depicts the ugly side of sharing and the promise of a dream home of one's own supported by a bank loan. Consequently, little is done to change the status quo.

While homeownership is still viewed as a central component of living out the American dream, presently many Americans are resisting customary living arrangements. One extreme example of this is vividly dramatised in *Nomadland*, the award-winning 2020 American film based on Jessica Bruder's non-fiction book *Nomadland: Surviving America in the Twenty-First Century*. A houseless, van-dwelling, working modern-day nomad travels and works, thereby exploring a life outside of conventional society. What is evident in the portrayal of this lifestyle is not only the hardship but also the freedom and the sense of community among the nomads.

Moreover, somewhat like in Medieval Europe, family members, relatives, neighbours and strangers are living communally in functional groups. People with whom they are sharing homes and lives are not just spouses or romantic partners, essentially a new form of kinship. The strong belief in the virtue of one-family, one-house means the benefits of sharing remain hidden and largely ignored, despite the steady erosion of traditional families and declining ability to afford homes.[28]

Co-housing developments are currently trending in cities: for example, StarCity, WeLive and Common are units in communal living complexes that can be rented in American cities. Being available on short-term leases allows for flexibility. Most units provide luxury amenities, such as laundry, maid service and gourmet kitchens: the facilities that many young people are seeking but cannot necessarily afford on their own. The Collective Old Oak Common, in London, is designed to offer residents many amenities. As well as apartments with shared communal areas, the project houses a co-working space, restaurant, gym, cinema, spa and launderette. While innovative, such developments are aimed at those with high incomes. Adaptation for the less affluent is called for. On a lighter side, German architects have suggested that Buckingham Palace with its 775 bedrooms and 78 bathrooms would be eminently suitable for co-residence.

As early as the mid-1980s, it was clear to Frances Baum[29] that fewer people were living in traditional households and she argued for greater acceptance and encouragement of alternatives. For example, couples' counselling is common but flatmate counselling is unheard of. Provision must be made to accommodate changing housing needs as evidence suggests that sharing is viable economically, socially and environmentally.

While the topic of flatting among young adults is relatively neglected, it no longer attracts the bad publicity and concern the communes of the 1960s did. Whereas older or married house sharers often encounter aversion to the sharing way of life, Sue Heath and Elizabeth Cleaver maintain that in the UK there is no shame attached to shared housing among contemporary young adults. Among younger adults, the lifestyle is frequently associated with privilege and tertiary qualifications. Heath and Cleaver suggested that previous research focused on deprived young people and failed to examine the everyday domestic lives of young adults. Consequently, little is known about this form of domesticity. Recently, the trend to ignore the domestic lives of youth has taken a turn for the better. For example, housing research has examined how the precariousness of enforced sharing with strangers in substandard housing impacts well-being and subverts any feeling that the accommodation is "home".[30]

We would argue that a contributing factor to the lack of research on shared housing is the transitory nature of this way of life. Considered a between style of housing, it has taken on a level of insignificance which, unfortunately, has ignored the fertile psychological ground this area offers for studying interpersonal relationships, group functioning, prejudice and discrimination and the role flatting plays in the process of becoming an independent adult.

Motivation for our research

The origins of our research interest lie in one of the authors overhearing a conversation between two young adult family members discussing the transparent and subtle ways in which their housemates discriminated against potential new flatmates. Subsequently, the authors investigated how young adults in New Zealand spoke about choosing prospective flatmates. This study led to a deep fascination and abiding intellectual curiosity about the broader dynamics involved in shared housing. Consistent with our earlier suggestions about how little was known about sharing, there was no academic literature on the topic of housemate choice. The data from this project suggested promising trajectories for further research. For example, the "flat dynamic" or "culture" was frequently employed as a rhetorical justification for determining the suitability of potential flatmates. Rather than explicitly discriminating based on factors such as age, race and unemployment, rejection was carefully framed in terms of compatibility with the existing flat dynamic. The concept "flat dynamic" was never explained or defined but comprehension was assumed.

This led to further research which sought to explore the meaning of such dynamics by looking in detail at the intricate social practices involved in this complex form of domesticity. Apart from the early study of communal living across the ages by Frances Baum and the seminal work on youth housing by Sue Heath and Elizabeth Cleaver, very little was known about the social benefits and costs of this way of life. Most research concentrated on *why* young people share.[31]

One aspect to be taken into consideration is the challenge involved in studying communal activity. There are several ways in which shared housing can be examined. For example, participants might agree to video cameras recording their everyday lives. Until now qualitative methods account for most research on young adult house sharing. Interviews have been the dominant research technique, using a range of methodologies from grounded theory to biographical interviewing.

Discourse analysis was chosen for our research, which sits at the heart of this book, as all experience and every human psychological phenomenon is integrated and interpreted in and through language. Human behaviour and social processes cannot be understood independently of language. Discursive psychologists regard language as the pivotal focus of inquiry and examine how people make sense of their worlds and themselves by employing hegemonic, pre-existing discourses that are available within their culture at a particular historical time. At micro- and macro-levels, the cultural, political and economic ideologies and social conditioning that powerfully affect lives can be discerned and can demonstrate how mundane talk is fundamentally linked to, constitutes and maintains broader social processes. For example, discursive psychologists have demonstrated the central role of language in all forms of prejudice and maintenance of oppression, despite the decrease in overt discrimination. By coincidence, the familialism discourse example that Ian Parker employs is relevant to this research. This discourse assumes, as natural, normal and universal, relationships operating within the heterosexual nuclear family and the gold standard against which all other ways of living should be measured and judged.[32] At the same time, discourses can also provide evidence of the complex processes of changing lifestyles that impact and are potently influenced by young adults.

While we have not included detailed discourse analysis in this book, it is useful to remember that our focus is on language. The primary goal of the research was to generate rich, complex accounts of how people describe their flatting experiences. What we report are the results of the analysis, which aimed at identifying key patterns in the data.

Data were obtained from semi-structured in-depth interviews with young adults who were flatting at the time. Interviews took place in 2010 and 2015. Participants were purposefully recruited by word of mouth. Participants were required to be fluent in English and between the ages of 20 and 35, with at least one year's flatting experience. The rationale for this was that those fairly new to flatting do not have insight born from experience. Twenty-four individuals were interviewed along with seven flat groups. Interviews were recorded and transcribed. Three flat group interviews were conducted in one of the major New Zealand cities and four in a provincial North Island town. The motivation for this choice was to increase heterogeneity and to assess if there were any differences between town and country.

Participants were Pākehā (New Zealanders of European descent) apart from two Māori, and two who identified as mixed Māori/Pākehā. There were 25 female and 16 male participants with a mean age of 24 years. The majority were university educated or students. Although most participants considered themselves professionals, one flat consisted of tradesmen and in another all were in retail. Variety, thus, entailed different combinations: all-male, all-female or mixed households.

Flat numbers ranged from two upwards. One individual interviewed had a staggering 21 flatmates. Pseudonyms are used to protect participants' identities.

Excerpts included in participants' talks are representative of commonly occurring discourses. Extracts retain the verbatim utterances of participants with little grammatical, syntax or punctuation corrections. Rather than complete sentences, natural breaks in the talk are indicated by moving to a new line.

Overview of following chapters

Chapter 2: We examine why the flatting lifestyle has extended well beyond student years. The increasingly recognised protracted transition to autonomous adulthood is discussed. Prolonged education has resulted not only in delaying entry into full-time employment but also in deferral of marriage and childbearing. Broad political, economic and social factors underlying this lengthier passage are considered as well as the waning stigma of singlehood. Single people are less likely to be able to live alone but are able to live full lives by sharing. Functional flats are positively regarded as "home" and flatmates are regarded as a family of choice. This has implications for reviewing the understanding of intimacy.

Chapter 3: We take an in-depth look at how young adults go about finding and choosing potential flatmates. Detailed results are presented of explanations and justifications offered for rejection or selection with respect to age, gender and ethnicity. While this raises the question of discrimination, it is important to find someone who will be most likely to fit in with the existing norms and mores of a household. In addition, we discuss attitudes to mental illness and substance abuse and what is regarded as acceptable or intolerable.

Chapter 4: We interrogate who makes the most desirable flatmates for successful co-residence. Preferences are for those who have interpersonal similarities and common expectations of each other. Trust and comfort with flatmates are essential as well as the need to be simultaneously independent and sufficiently sociable. These desirable requirements provide valuable insight into why individuals may discriminate against prospective flatmates. Additional overlays that arose were around the issues of living with friends or strangers and whether couples or singles were preferred.

Chapter 5: By focusing on the economic reasons for flatting, it is easy to lose sight of the well-documented social advantages the lifestyle can afford. Can expectations of equal sharing of household chores undermine the positive interpersonal aspects of house sharing? In addition, we examine the effectiveness of rosters. Rosters have been mooted as a safe way of overcoming problems with domestic chores but our research suggests that rosters are ineffective and are regarded as counterproductive to freedom and autonomy.

Chapter 6: Household chores have commonly been identified as a major source of conflict. This chapter explores further areas of conflict and considers how conflict is best managed as well as the negative repercussions of unresolvable problems. Additionally, we consider the social environment alongside the physical environment and the impact the building lived in can have on relationships.

Chapter 7: This chapter looks at the social dynamics of shared living. The intricate workings of successful flats are put under the microscope as we consider how things work, the importance of a good fit among flatmates and the need to respect a number of balances and the tensions that can arise if these fall out of kilter. The chapter begins with additional topics that arose in the talk but were not particularly common or dominant but contribute to increasing understanding of sharing. The chapter ends with two further considerations that can affect domestic relationships: household numbers and uneven power balance.

Chapter 8: The concluding chapter reiterates the significance of social psychological research in the everyday domestic lives of young adults. Whereas this book deals with relatively privileged young adults with good education and career prospects, recent research by sociologists, urban planners and policy makers has concentrated on young people at the lower end of income scales. Since our participants find themselves unable to afford living solo then the plight of the more vulnerable is less positive. We briefly summarise our findings and tidy up some loose ends. Our contribution to the slowly but steadily growing data on the topic is discussed as well as its shortcomings. Suggestions are made for future study of the topic.

Notes

1 Rebecca Williamson, "Flatting Futures: Negotiating Domesticity, Home and Individuality in the New Zealand Flat," Unpublished Master's Thesis. Victoria University, 2006.

2 Annie E. Casey Foundation, "What We Know About Youth and Young Adult Homelessness," March 2, 2021, www.aecf.org/blog/what-we-know-about-youth-and-young-adult-homelessness.

3 Bob Day, "The Politics of Housing Affordability: A Contrived Crisis," *12th Annual Demographia International Housing Affordability Survey*, 2016, http://demographia.com/dhi2016.pdf; George Friedman, "The Global Impact of a US Recession," *Geopolitical Futures*, March 26, 2019, https://geopoliticalfutures.com/global-impact-us-recession-1/; Julie Rugg and Deborah Quilgars, "Young People and Housing: A Review of the Present Policy and Practice Landscape," *Youth & Policy Special Edition* 114 (2015): 5–16; Gill Jones, "Experimenting with Households and Inventing Homes," *International Social Science Journal* 164 (2000): 183–194.

4 Rowan Arundel and Richard Ronald, "Parental Co-residence, Shared Living and Emerging Adulthood in Europe: Semi-Dependent Housing Across Welfare Regime and Housing System Contexts," *Journal of Youth Studies* 19 (2016); Massimo Bricocoli and Stephania Sabatinelli, "House Sharing Amongst Young Adults in the Context of Mediterranean Welfare: The Case of Milan," *International Journal of Housing Policy* 16, no. 2 (2016): 184–200; Laryssa Mykyta and Suzanne Macartney, "Sharing a Household: Household Composition and Economic Well-Being: 2007–2010," *US Census Bureau: Current Population Report* (2012): 60–242, www.census.gov/prod/2012pubs/p60-242; Jason Hilder, Elin Charles-Edwards, Thomas Sigler and Bill Metcalfe, "Housemates, Inmates and Living Mates: Communal Living in Australia," *Australian Planner* 55, no. 1 (2018): 12–27; Rebecca Williamson, "Flat Food: Food, Sociability and the Individual in the New Zealand Flat," *New Zealand Sociology* 20 (2005): 4–17.

5 Annette Steinführer and Annegret Haase, "Flexible-Inflexible: Socio-Demographic, Spatial and Temporary Dimensions of Flat Sharing in Leipzig, Germany," *Geo Journal* 74 (2009): 567–587; Frances Goldscheider and Calvin Goldscheider, *Ethnicity, Familism and Generational Relationships* (Madison, WI: University of Wisconsin Press, 1993); Kristen Natalier, "I'm Not His Wife": Doing Gender in Share Households," Unpublished

Doctoral Thesis. University of Queensland, 2003; Kristen Natalier, "Independence, Individualism & Connection Among Share Householders," *Youth Studies Australia* 26, no. 1 (2007): 17–24; Sophie McNamara and John Connell, "Homeward Bound: Searching for Home in Inner City Share Houses," *Australian Geographer* 38 (2007): 71–91; Rebecca Williamson, "Flatting Futures"; Sue Heath and Elizabeth Cleaver, *Young, Free and Single? Twenty-Somethings and Household Change* (Hampshire: Palgrave Macmillan, 2003).

6 For example, Oana Druta, Richard Ronald and Sue Heath, "Urban Singles and Shared Housing," *Social & Cultural Geography* 22, no. 9 (2021): 1195–1203; Kim McKee, Adriana Mihaela Soaita and Jennifer Hoolachan, "'Generation Rent' and the Emotions of Private Renting: Self-Worth, Status and Insecurity Amongst Low-Income Renters," *Housing Studies* 35, no. 8 (2020): 1468–1487.

7 Annamarie Pluhar, *Sharing Housing: A Guidebook for Finding and Keeping Good Housemates* (East Dummerston, VT: Homemate Publishing, 2011); Lauren Earl, *Flatter's Survival Guide* (Wellington: Awa Press, 2013); Tanya Sassoon, *Flatmate Survival Handbook* (Great Britain: Bloomsbury, 2007).

8 John Birmingham, *He Died With a Falafel in His Hand* (Sydney: Duffy & Snellgrove, 2001).

9 Sue Heath, Katherine Davies, Gemma Edwards and Rachel M. Scicluna, *Shared Housing, Shared Lives: Everyday Experiences Across the Lifecourse* (London: Routledge, 2019).

10 Jonathan Potter, "Discourse Analysis and Constructionist Approaches: Theoretical Background," in *Handbook of Qualitative Research Methods for Psychology and the Social Sciences*, ed John T. E. Richardson (Leicester: BPS Books, 1996), 125–140, 135.

11 Rachael Scicluna, *Home and Sexuality: The Other Side of the Kitchen* (London: Palgrave Macmillan, 2017).

12 Ilana E. Strauss, "The Hot New Millennial Housing Trend Is a Repeat of the Middle Ages," The Atlantic, September 26, 2016, https://www.theatlantic.com/business/archive/2016/09/millennial-housing-communal-living-middle-ages/501467/.

13 Bella DePaulo, *How We Live Now: Redefining Home and Family in the 21st Century* (New York: Atria Books, 2015).

14 Heath and Cleaver, *Young, Free and Single.*

15 Deborah A. Cobb-Clark, "Leaving Home: What Economics Has to Say About the Living Arrangements of Young Australians," *Australian Economic Review* 41 (2008): 60–172; Joce Stewart, Sue Floyd and Shona Thompson, "The Way We Were: Collegiality in Nursing in the '70s and '80s," *Kai Tiaki Nursing Research* 6 (2015): 4–9.

16 Shirley Ayres, "The Ghost of Curran Street," *New Zealand Memories* 104 (2013): 14.

17 James K. Baxter, "A Small Ode on Mixed Flatting," in *Collected Poems*, ed John Edward Weir (Wellington: Oxford University Press, 1979), 396–399. Reprinted with permission from the Estate of James K. Baxter.

18 Malcolm Harris and Neal Gorenflo, eds., *Share or Die: Voices of the Get Lost Generation in the Age of Crisis* (Gabriola: New Society Publishers, 2012); Katherine Burn and Cassandra Szoek, "Boomerang Families and Failure-to-Launch: Commentary on Adult Children Living at Home," *Maturitas* 83 (2016): 9–12; Wojtek Tomaszewski, Jonathan F. Smith, Cameron Parsell, Bruce Tranter, Jacqueline Laughland-Booÿ and Zlatko Skrbiš, "Young, Anchored and Free? Examining the Dynamics of Early Housing Pathways in Australia," *Journal of Youth Studies* 20, no. 7 (2017): 904–926.

19 Natalier, "I'm Not His Wife"; Sally Cameron, *Edmonds' Food for Flatters* (Auckland: Hodder Moa Beckett, 2003); Sally Cameron, *Edmonds' More Food for Flatters* (Auckland: Hodder Moa Beckett, 2007).

20 Arundel and Ronald, "Parental Co-residence"; Fatoş Gökşen, Deniz Yükseker, Alpay Filiztekin, İbrahim Öker, Sinem Kuz, Fernanda Mazzotta and Lavinia Parisi, "Leaving and Returning to the Parental Home During the Economic Crisis," *STYLE Working Papers WP8.3, CROME*, University of Brighton, Brighton (2016), www.style-research.eu/publications.

21 Erik Stenberg, *Structural Systems of the Million Program Era* (Stockholm: KTH School of Architecture, 2013).

22 Allie Volpe, "The Strange, Unique Intimacy of the Roommate Relationship," *The Atlantic*, August 14, 2018, www.theatlantic.com/family/archive/2018/08/the-strange-unique-intimacy-of-the-roommate-relationship/567296/; Anglicare Rental Affordability Snapshot, April 2021, www.anglicare.asn.au/wp-content/uploads/2021/05/rental-affordability-snapshot-national-report.pdf.
23 Jennifer Hoolachan, Kim McKee, Tom Moore and Adriana Mihaela, "'Generation Rent' and the Ability to 'Settle Down': Economic and Geographical Variation in Young People's Housing Transitions," *Journal of Youth Studies* 20 (2017): 63–78; Darrin Hodgetts, Kerry Chamberlain, Shiloh Groot and Yardena Tankel, "Urban Poverty, Structural Violence and Welfare Provision for 100 Families in Auckland," *Urban Studies* 51, no. 10 (2014): 2036–2051.
24 Natalier, "I'm Not His Wife."
25 DePaulo, *How We Live Now*.
26 Karsten Mause, "The Tragedy of the Commune: Learning From the Worst-Case Scenarios," *Journal of Socio-Economics* 37, no. 1 (2008): 308–327.
27 Sherry Ahrentzen, "Double Indemnity or Double Delight? The Health Consequences of Shared Housing and 'Doubling Up'," *Journal of Social Issues* 59 (2003): 547–568.
28 Heath et al., *Shared Housing, Shared Lives*; DePaulo, *How We Live Now*.
29 Frances Baum, "Shared Housing: Making Alternative Lifestyles Work," *Australian Journal of Social Issues* 24 (1986): 197–212.
30 Heath and Cleaver, "Young, Free and Single"; Elinor Wilkinson and Ilana Ortega-Alcázar, "Stranger Danger? The Intersectional Impacts of Shared Housing on Young People's Health & Wellbeing," *Health & Place* 60 (2019): 102–191; McKee, Soaita and Hoolachan, "'Generation Rent' and the Emotions of Private Renting."
31 Baum, "Shared Housing"; Heath and Cleaver, "Young, Free and Single."
32 Ian Parker, *Discourse Dynamics: Critical Analysis for Social and Individual Psychology* (London: Routledge, 1992).

2

WHY YOUNG ADULTS ARE FLATTING WELL BEYOND STUDENT YEARS

House sharing among young adults, particularly in Commonwealth countries, is a pragmatic response to changing economic, political and social circumstances. Epic changes have resulted in protracted and varying pathways to autonomous adulthood in contemporary young adults. Here we examine the factors underlying the lengthier transition to adulthood and the increasing attraction of remaining single for longer than previous generations, if not indefinitely. Since successful shared households are regarded as home, we consider the notion that sharing can be seen as a family of choice. Consequently, understanding domestic intimacy requires reassessment.

Protracted transitions to adulthood of contemporary youth

Youth researchers propose that adulthood no longer begins when adolescence ends. Young adults stay in school longer than previous generations. They also tend to delay marriage and having children. These and other factors contribute to an extended period of transition to adulthood which has, for example, been referred to as "post adolescence" by Manuela du Bois-Reymond and "emerging adulthood" by Jeffrey Arnett. The protracted progression frequently lasts throughout the twenties and even extends into the thirties with many personal, professional and emotional issues in a state of flux and change. Jeffrey Arnett maintains that this period is characterised by five features: identity exploration; instability; self-focus; feelings of in-between and possibilities. While these are universal features, they are more common during emerging adulthood than in other life stages.[1]

Parallels of this posited pre-adult phase are drawn with the emergence and recognition of adolescence as a distinct life stage. In the early twentieth century agricultural economies, where children were vital labour, changed to industrialisation.

DOI: 10.4324/9781003161370-2

Schooling in the Western world became the norm because children were not suited to employment in industry and industrial wages for men were sufficient to cover education for their children. The altered pattern of a seemingly seamless progress from childhood to adulthood, characteristic of pre-industrial society, left many young people in the ambivalent state of being neither an adult nor a child. In 1904, Granville Stanley Hall suggested the term "adolescence" to describe the period as a distinct life phase, a semi-autonomous state, which enabled young people to be educated for longer, explore employment options and create a self-identity. Notably, Hall suggested adolescence could last up to the age of 25. Similar to this change in the early twenty-first century, a unique transition stage is materialising that can largely be attributed to lengthier periods spent in higher education and more young adults entering post-secondary education and training to prepare for economic independence.[2]

The declining availability of traditional occupations, typical of post-war industrialisation, advances in technology and uncertainty of future employment have dramatically increased the demand and standards for skilled labour in the last half century.[3] Protracted, lengthy periods of professional and technical training are a necessity rather than a choice but do not necessarily guarantee well-paying work.

Prolonged education has resulted not only in delaying entry into full-time employment but also in deferral of marriage and childbearing. By the end of the Second World War, economic self-sufficiency, marriage and parenting occurred soon after the end of schooling. However, such early marriage is now the exception. The current marital age reflects earlier pre-World War trends. The difference is that in the past most single people lived with their parents until marriage. Today, acceptance of premarital sex, co-habitation and easy access to birth control has rendered early marriage less desirable.[4] While transitioning to adulthood currently involves a period of living independently, leaving the parental home is not as final as it once was.

The dominant theory in developmental psychology regarding young adults is incorporated in Erikson's eight stages of psycho-social development. This proposes that early adulthood, in which lasting relationships and career commitments are made, starts in the late teens and ends in the adolescent phase beginning with puberty. While Erikson acknowledged that there are significantly different cultural dimensions to adolescence, his theory may no longer represent a normative pattern: seriously settling into occupations, professions and partnerships is being postponed for many. Importantly, different paths can be expected across cultures, circumstances and gender. Timing patterns are diverse, less orderly and less predictable.[5]

In most countries, the legal rights and responsibilities of adulthood, such as voting, drinking and driving, are explicitly structured by age. Not without debate about how early they should be granted, they have remained fairly static. While 86% of countries have 18 as the legal age required to register to vote, there are variations. In Scotland, the age is 16 and on the other extreme the United Arab Emirates has the age at 25. These important legal ages for the commencement of particular adult responsibilities are supported by other less formal markers such as finishing education; stable, full-time employment; economic self-sufficiency; marriage and parenting. While financial independence from parents tied to psychological perceptions of autonomy remains a significant marker in the transition to adulthood, they are no longer central to a definition of adulthood. Kristen Natalier speaks of an ambiguous dependency where young people are still partially reliant on parents financially, yet other measures, such as living away from home, taking responsibility for actions, autonomous decision making, developing an adult relationship with parents and deciding on personal beliefs are important in advancing to adult status and empowerment.[6]

In recent times, the average ages for marriage and beginning a family have shifted by almost a decade. In 1971, when marriage rates peaked in New Zealand, the median age at first marriage was 23.0 years for men and 20.8 years for women. In 2018, the median age at first marriage or civil union was 30.4 years for men and 29.2 years for women, compared with 28.6 and 26.7, respectively, in 1998. Although the median age at first marriage has increased over the last 20 years, most of the increase occurred before 2004. A similar picture is evident when considering mothers' ages when their first child was born. In 1968, the median birth age for a first child for mothers was 23.39; this increased to 30 years in 1999 and has remained fairly static since then. In 2018, the median age of mothers at the birth of their first child in New Zealand was 30.5 years. New Zealand figures are closely mirrored by statistics in Australia. Similar figures are cited in the UK, and in the USA the average age of marriage has been trending upwards: according to 2018 statistics, the average age at which women get married is 27.8 years, and for men, the average age of marriage is 29.8 years.[7]

Robin Goodwin argues that current changes will be impacted by and be subject to future change. While change is regarded by some as a linear progress with contemporary society having achieved the highest level, change can be seen as a more cyclical progress. Nevertheless, sociologists have cautioned that the full socio-economic ramifications of this protracted period have yet to be understood. Life courses, formally dictated by the dominant narratives of social institutions, such as the church, family and culture no longer prevail. Gender, which was one of the main factors in structuring life stages, is losing its determining influence. Education levels among women continue to rise with increased participation in and commitment to the labour market, reducing reliance on husbands for economic security. Marriage is no longer necessary for women's legal and social status. Education has not only opened doors for women to many professions and civic life previously dominated by men but a career is seen as an attractive alternative or delay to early marriage and child-rearing.[8]

The waning influence of religion and secularisation of society has resulted in changes in social conventions relating to sexual practices. Together with easily obtainable birth control methods and legalised abortion reducing unwanted pregnancies, marriage and even co-habitation can be less attractive to women. There are advantages to sexual freedom for young adults in their own domestic space without the demands of living with a partner even though most young adults eventually aspire to a couple household.

As early as 1986, Linda Waite and colleagues considered the possibility that the distinctly diverse passage to adulthood, free of family obligations and constraints, could considerably impact later lives: co-habitation can provide the benefits of intimacy and economy with fewer expectations of asymmetric gender roles.[9] The trend to later coupling and childbearing adds to the sense of flexibility around the edges of transitioning into the adult world with clear implications for the business of sharing households. In addition, relationship status no longer defines individuals; remaining unmarried is now less likely to be regarded as a lack of options but more as a lifestyle choice.

While there is a popular stereotype of young single adults feeling somehow left out of the paired society made up of happy couples, this is far from universally so. Indeed, many are in no rush to relinquish the freedom and joys of independent young adulthood. The mass divorces of post-World War generations may have much to do with many young people carefully considering marriage before making commitments. There is a greater awareness of the personal costs and restraints associated with traditional households, which are not always idyllic or safe havens. In addition, the heterosexual assumptions implicit in these norms are questioned. Both men and women are hesitant to relinquish their economic and individual independence and are less optimistic about the classic nuclear family. Sex, emotional intimacy and support do not necessarily entail marriage, co-habitation or dependence.

The twenty-first century has been designated as *the singles century* but privileging of marriage persists. Single people remain stereotyped as lonely and unfulfilled but the singlehood stigma is waning. The indignity of single women, cruelly referred to as old maids, having to reside with parents or married siblings no longer applies. As the possibilities of living a full and meaningful life become more widely accepted, remaining unmarried may become more of a genuine choice. Those marrying will do so if it is a lifestyle they desire not because of social prescription.[10]

Single folk are financially able to live their own lives, very often by sharing households with non-kin and unencumbered by family rules and restraints. Sharing is not regarded solely as a transitional stopgap or problematic but as financially and socially pragmatic.

Motivation for sharing households

Since young adults are often the shock absorbers of economic reform, they are frequently both the driving force for accommodating and shaping social, political and economic changes. Shared domestic living arrangements are one way of negotiating change. While adapting to economic constraints is important in understanding new household formations, this may also be the incentive for transforming collaborative living into a popular and successful form of accommodation. Sharing is a domestic arrangement particularly suited to young people strongly committed to the labour force. Flatting affords a professional standard of accommodation, which would be impossible on a single salary. Very often students, accustomed to shared living, continue flatting once they graduate.

In the UK, Elizabeth Kenyon and Sue Heath found significant narratives of choice for this lifestyle, beyond the student years. In the USA, sharing is a growing trend among people beyond college age, and underlying the economic aspect is the feeling that companionship is good and privacy overrated. Annamarie Pluhar feels that the pervasive myth of the self-reliant independent person is being challenged by the companionship and shared responsibility of sharing.[11]

Conversely, Eric Klinenberg extolls the virtues of "singleton" living, while simultaneously acknowledging that it can be a lonely and isolating experience for some. Preferences for solo living are attributed to emphasis on independence and other features of late capitalism, such as individualism, increasing globalisation and urbanisation as well as digital economics. Shared domesticity may not be a way of life suited to all, but for some living alone in a one-person household is not desirable. In addition, not all single people have the economic resources to live on their own.[12] Our research contributes to this debate by aligning positively on the side of communal living.

Lucy, in her mid-thirties, who works in the banking sector, speaks of the dual attractions of sharing.

> *Why do I flat? Well for budget reasons.*
> *it's cheaper, it's more affordable*
> *so where I'm living now which is close to town*
> *if I was to live by myself*
> *it would cost quite a lot of money*
> *and then I also like the social side of it*
> *cooking for other people is great*
> *and that kind of interaction.*
> *I think probably [those] would be the two main drivers.*

Aside from economy and companionship, location is important to young folk. Proximity to work and the attraction of inner-city life are desirable but are currently extremely costly in terms of real estate and rent. Phoebe, in her early thirties, who works for an office temping agency, also highlights the social aspect of flatting.

> *Even if I was in the position to have my own place*
> *I think I'd still want to flat*
> *because of the social aspect of it*
> *you know being able to come home*
> *have a chat with someone about your crappy day*
> *that social aspect I think I'd miss*
> *because I have lived on my own in the UK*
> *for a little while and it's quite lonely*
> *even if you have an active social life it can still be nice*
> *to have that someone to hang out with*

Phoebe stresses the loneliness of living in a one-person household while simultaneously acknowledging the financial imperative.

Economic factors

Financial constraint is the dominant motivation for the prevalence and extended tenure of flatting. Young people are typically stretched financially with shared housing, one of the few remaining viable accommodation options for young adults in cities. Significantly, the extended tenure of flatting was before the 2008 economic crisis, and currently, the outlook post-Brexit and COVID-19 remains uncertain. Quite simply, two or more people are able to live more cheaply by sharing costs of accommodation, power, broadband, etc.

Sue Heath and Elizabeth Cleaver cite the ongoing British government policies within the fields of education, training, employment and housing as significantly impacting young adults in contemporary society. This is compounded by deteriorating economic conditions and insecurity in the labour market. In addition, the ongoing austerity measures have resulted in diminishing social housing and conditional access to welfare.[13] The effects of public policy on the lives of young people are also evident in America, Australia and New Zealand.[14]

Cost of education and work training

Conditions faced by young adults today differ from the baby boom generation. Work training, such as nursing, teaching and apprenticeships, in the past in New Zealand, was accompanied by a wage and often low-cost, subsidised housing and a confident expectation of full-employment on training completion. Post-secondary education was relatively free, with student allowances for almost all students. In the 1980s, New Zealand adopted a market-based approach to tertiary education as part of an overall reaction to changing economic conditions. What was previously regarded as a socially elitist education system was replaced by a system of mass participation in higher education beginning in 1985, the cost of which was increasingly borne by students themselves. In 1989, the Labour Government introduced university tuition fees for all and financial assistance was strictly targeted. Student loans were introduced in 1992 and universities were permitted to set their own fees.[15] These changes in policy combined with escalating and prolonged education costs have seen an unprecedented number of young people leaving tertiary institutions with huge debt.

The increase in student loans has been driven by rising fees but even more so by restrictions on allowances, forcing more and more students to borrow to live from week to week. Even with the current free first year of tertiary education, the situation is unparalleled in history: the magnitude of debt would have been more than adequate for a house deposit in past decades. It has been argued that in the long run graduates are not adversely affected if they manage their debt well. Graduates may acquire human capital, abilities and skills through investment in education and training with potentially increased salaries, but in the short term their take-home pay is greatly reduced by having to pay off student loans. With student debt substantially mounting, graduates are taking longer to pay back the money they owe. The median forecast repayment time for borrowers who finished study in 2016 was 5.8 years.[16] When the full-time workforce is entered, there is less disposable income and hence more likelihood of the need to share.

Housing unaffordability

Added to the financial pressures produced by student loan debt, significant problems with housing affordability and the extended housing price boom in New Zealand have made house buying for young people increasingly difficult. Restricted purchasing power is not confined to New Zealand. Steffen Wetzstein predicted another international crisis following the GFC: a Global Urban Housing Affordability Crisis.[17] Salary and wage increases are not keeping pace with housing-related household expenses. In many urban centres around the world, neo-liberal housing policies have resulted in the commodification of residential housing skewed towards higher returns on investments. State-assisted options are scarce.

Between 1986 and 2006, the largest fall in home ownership rates was in the 25–39 age range. Home ownership rates for young New Zealanders have declined drastically since 1990. Home ownership rate for young people aged 25–34 in 2001 was 38%. By 2018, this dropped to 30%.[18] There is now a generation of graduates who struggle to afford houses, especially in the major New Zealand cities. For many talented young people, moving to smaller towns in order to get on the property ladder or without crippling mortgage rates means they may well not reach their professional potential, or even find suitable employment. One option is for extended commuting to larger centres. While home ownership, believed to encourage self-reliance and good citizenship, has been central to New Zealand culture and socio-political stability, evidence points to home ownership among the younger age groups being less likely than ever. And this is keenly felt by young adults who grew up with the expectation of being able to buy a home in the early stage of their careers. The following extract comes from 26-year-old chef, Max:

> *When I got into flatting that was about the time*
> *that people began to realise our generation are the ones*
> *well we're maybe going to be the ones who*
> *are going be renting their flat for their entire life*
> *and not be able to afford their own home*

The diminishing gap between home ownership aspirations and confidence in achieving this is by no means confined to New Zealand. Young people are renting and sharing for longer periods, which may last a lifetime, giving rise to the term "Generation Rent".[19] Many previous generations had the benefit of government home ownership loans from the State Advances Corporation. Housing prices after the 2008 global financial crisis have increased dramatically, and while interest rates are at historically low levels credit access for housing has tightened and local council rates continue to rise. The undersupply of housing, especially in the lower-priced market sector, puts pressure on the rental sector and can be expected to continue since the building industry remains primarily focused on the middle and higher end of the housing market, geared towards nuclear families.

Together with positive net migration, these factors increase the cost and affordability of housing and ensure a lack of suitable housing for youth on entry-level incomes. Since the housing market does not accommodate the needs of the young, they need to shape their needs to fit what is available. Flatting is an economically viable means of sharing resources which enable young adults to save for their own homes and more immediate aspirations, such as travel. Renting and house sharing also provide pragmatic and flexible choices for young adults with vocational ambition, who need to be highly mobile to succeed in a competitive employment market. And it needs to be reiterated here that our research focuses on relatively affluent young adults: housing security and prospects for those on social welfare, partially employed or minimum wage are more bleak.

Competitive labour market

The nature of the labour market, in which workers compete for employment and employees compete for workers, affects national trends and this is the driving force behind many changes in society. There have been significant revisions to the nature of labour markets in recent decades, which particularly impact youth, including the shift from manufacturing to a service economy, and decreased demand for unskilled workers. New communication technologies and the globalisation of the economy, with attendant growing business competition, pressurise businesses to reduce staff and costs resulting in a reduced commitment to and protection of workers. Entire industries are exported to developing countries, where there are low wages and fewer human rights, with huge job losses in Western countries. Corporations have embraced the technological displacement of workers by computers and robots, making many people redundant and downsizing of the workforce.[20]

To succeed in increasingly competitive and volatile labour markets, and achieve a stable position in the working world, young people require a high degree of geographic flexibility without being tied to a particular location. Transitional employment is characteristic of the early stages of establishing a career. In New Zealand, the under-thirties are the workers most likely to change jobs to gain better pay and training opportunities: secure tenure tends to increase with age as people become better paid. This makes it difficult for young people to put down roots and form attachments to places in which they live. Platonic friendships let alone couple relationships are harder to maintain. Lasting partnerships become increasingly difficult without compromise, sacrifice and considerable stress. When moving cities or countries, shared accommodation can offer access to a ready-made social life through flatmates and can provide protection from the possibility of loneliness. As Sue Heath suggests, by adhering to the idea that shared housing is essentially a product of economic constraint we lose sight of the fact this might not be the sole precipitating factor. It has been suggested that functional shared accommodation operates as a surrogate "family" of choice, providing a sanctuary of companionship, support and security with strong social and emotional attachments.[21] This leads to consideration of alternative modes of families, home and intimacy.

Redefining families, home and intimacy

Families of choice

Traditionally, the family and deeply rooted kinship ties have been the foundation of Western society. The word "family" has potent social, cultural and symbolic connotations and denotes a kinship relationship by blood, adoption or marriage. But the boundaries of what constitutes "family" are becoming increasingly fluid in complex ways with blurring between kin, non-kin and ex-kin. In the past few decades, "family" has become a contested term as it has taken on a much broader egalitarian and diverse form than the customary association with heterosexual marriage. Rachael Scicluna observes that the family is an ideological, rather than a functional unit. There is a need for greater recognition of variations of families and an intellectual shift from the conventional concept of "family".[22]

Judith Stacey coined the term "post-modern families" to describe the diverse, elective, non-kin relationships based on friendship and commitments that characterise families of choice. Media recognition of these differing households is reflected in the American television comedy, *Modern Family*. In 2019, the sitcom *Friends* celebrated 25 years since it first aired. In an article on its popularity, entitled *Friends: The show that changed our idea of family*, Clare Thorpe wrote that this alternative family life introduced a new type of domesticity into the mainstream spectrum of normalcy. Looking to friends for support resonated with many.[23]

Whatever the family pattern there is a sense of belonging, commitment and emotional support, and apart from young children some form of shared responsibility is expected. Research has emphasised that supportive relationships are a key meaning of home but these have been largely understood and conflated with marriage and nuclear family relationships. Family-based households have continued to prevail in the face of competition in widely different eras and across sociological environments. The values and comfort associated with the family unit have often failed to materialise in traditional families and can be places of physical, psychological and emotional abuse. Nevertheless, they have been adopted by families of choice, perhaps because conventional households do have intrinsic merits. Rising divorce rates, single parenting, co-habitation, deferred marriage and single-sex unions are all indicative of profound, irrevocable moral change and the emergence of increasingly flexible and fluid modes of intimacy. And changes lead to gradual transformation in beliefs and values.

The terms "family" and "home" have been employed synonymously. Sophie McNamara and John Connell's study sought to enlarge cultural and social understandings of "home" by examining the extent to which shared households replicate or challenge the tradition of the "family home". In so doing, they consider the way shared living may be a significant and meaningful experience for occupants. Possibly, the impermanence of flatting households subverts their recognition as a home and family. The conflation of home and the nuclear family is outdated. There is a need to re-evaluate and challenge what constitutes family and question the concept of home to different people. Just as predictable life paths have become more fractured, the meaning of home has become more fluid.[24]

Bella DePaulo writes about changing definitions of home and family in the twenty-first century. Within this dynamic landscape a dazzling array of contemporary living arrangements are identified. These include, and also go beyond, the simple notions of the nuclear family occupying a single household and a single home dweller living alone. Mostly these living arrangements involve people sharing, such as young adults (boomerang children) living with parents, older adults living with their middle-aged children, siblings and other relatives sharing, and unrelated adults sharing.[25] Shared housing challenges the straightforward ideology of the nuclear family as the correct and only way to live. Redefining home also means reassessing relationships.

The changing nature of intimacy

Acknowledgement of alternatives to the heterosexual nuclear family is a relatively recent phenomenon, primarily associated with research on relationships and household patterns among homosexual couples. With increasing recognition of the viability of once unacceptable or marginal types of relationships, a greater understanding of new possibilities of intimacy is called for. Personal relationships today go beyond marriage and blood ties with commitments extending the boundaries of the nuclear, co-resident family. Love, trust and care are not limited to families: they can characterise friendships and other social networks. Fragmentation of traditional families has meant a greater reliance on friendships as a source of security. Different forms of bonds, whether they be physical, emotional, spiritual or emotional, are significant. Sue Heath and colleagues have demonstrated that shared domestic living friendships can create connections that are intimate, supportive and emotionally meaningful in a time when lifetime employment, relationships and family living nearby are no longer guaranteed. Shared housing weakens the boundaries of public and private spaces between friends and promotes a high degree of intimacy and interdependence.[26]

Arguably, the media appear to be far faster at feeling the pulse of change than social scientists. Different modes of intimacy are recognised and reflected in many popular, but already dated television shows, such as *Friends, Will and Grace* and *Sex in the City*. Yet heteronormative relationships remain institutionalised and society still operates as though traditional families predominate with new forms of relationships often derided, trivialised and subordinated to conventional relationships.[27] Bella DePaulo notes that "while 'family' is still sentimentalized . . . it may be friendship rather than family that captures the essence of the 21st Century".[28] Protective policy and legislation lag behind irrevocable changes perhaps due to the threatening powers of new ways of life, which risk violating accepted ways of living.

Sue Heath and Elizabeth Cleaver suggest that modern youths are transforming the boundaries of interpersonal relationships, looking to their friends rather than sexual partners or family to meet immediate needs for intimacy. Giddens' "pure love" is not restricted to sexuality, with intimacy described as "a transactional negotiation of personal ties by equals", which can be descriptive of shared domestic arrangements among non-kin young adults.[29] This does not rule out sexual relationships developing but requires new negotiations of boundaries. This transformation of intimacy was somewhat evident in our research, where Laura, an otherwise articulate project manager in her early thirties, struggled to express her feelings:

> *I guess it's almost like a boyfriend or girlfriend*
> *in some respects, because you have to like them on a personal level*
> *because you are living with them and*
> *you know you have a home together*

The quality and intimacy of the relationship are of particular importance in the construction and meaning of the modern family. Once the teenage years are reached, family loyalties decline to be replaced by group identity and social belonging. Friends have consistently been demonstrated to be of the greatest importance in the lives of contemporary young adults. Sharing a household with someone at some point in life extends beyond school friendships and increases the odds of being considered a family member. Laura's statement has definite implications that shared domesticity means that members of a flat share a "home" together not merely a roof overhead. Sharing is therefore significant beyond a simple accommodation option.

Conclusion

In this chapter, we have located the popularity of flatting in New Zealand and the English-speaking Western world within the context of changing economic and social conditions. These alterations have produced a prolonged transitional phase to adulthood. Economic factors include lengthening of the education process, instability in the labour market and lack of affordable housing. Socially, these include the rise of co-habitation, relaxation of sexual norms, legalised abortion and contraception and gender equality in education and employment. All can contribute to delayed marriage and childbearing. We briefly discussed new definitions of intimacy and families. The next chapter examines the choice of potential flatmates.

Notes

1 Manuela du Bois-Reymond, "'I Don't Want to Commit Myself Yet': Young People's Life Concepts," *Journal of Youth Studies* 1 (1998): 63–79; Jeffrey J. Arnett, *Emerging Adulthood: A Theory of Adulthood From the Late Teens Through the Twenties*, 2nd ed. (Oxford: Oxford University Press, 2015).

2 Frank F. Furstenberg, Ruben G. Rumbaut and Richard A. Settersten, "On the Frontier of Adulthood: Emerging Themes and New Directions," in *On the Frontier of Adulthood: Theory, Research and Public Policy*, eds Frank F. Furstenberg, Ruben G. Rumbaut and Richard A. Settersten (Chicago, IL: Chicago University Press, 2005), 1–3; Granville Stanley Hall, *Adolescence: Its Psychology and Its Relation to Physiology, Anthropology, Sociology, Sex, Crime, Religion, and Education* (Englewood Cliffs, NJ: Prentice Hall, 1904), https://archive.org/details/adolescenceitsps002hall; Arnett, *Emerging Adulthood.*

3 Kerwin Kofi Charles, Erik Hurst and Matthew J. Notowidigdo, "The Masking of the Decline in Manufacturing Employment by the Housing Bubble," *Journal of Economic Perspectives* 30, no. 2 (2016): 179–200.

4 Jeremy Greenwood and Nezih Guner, "Social Change: The Sexual Revolution," *PSC Working Paper Series* 12 (2009), https://repository.upenn.edu/psc_working_papers/12.

5 Erik H. Erikson, "Eight Ages of Man," *International Journal of Psychiatry* 2 (1966): 281–300; Marcia C. Inhorn and Nancy J. Smith-Hefner, eds., *Waithood: Gender, Education, and Global Delays in Marriage and Childbearing* (Oxford: Berghahn Books, 2020); Andy Furlong, *Youth Studies: An Introduction* (London: Routledge, 2013).

6 Sharon Omondi, "Legal Voting Age by Country," *Politics*, September 7, 2017, www.worldatlas.com/articles/legal-voting-age-by-country.html; Kristen Natalier, "Independence, Individualism & Connection among Share Householders," *Youth Studies Australia* 26 (2007): 17–24.

7 Statistics New Zealand, Marriages, Civil Unions, and Divorces: Year ended December 2018, www.stats.govt.nz/information-releases/marriages-civil-unions-and-divorces-year-ended-december-2020; Australian Bureau of Statistics, *Marriages and Divorces Australia*, 2020, www.abs.gov.au; Gary R. Lee and Krista K. Payne, "Changing Marriage Patterns Since 1970: What's Going On, and Why?," *Journal of Comparative Family Studies* 41, no. 4 (2010): 537–555; Sally C. Curtin and Paul D. Sutton, "Marriage Rates in the United States, 1900–2018," *NCHS Health E-Stat*, 2020, https://www.cdc.gov/nchs/data/hestat/marriage_rate_2018/marriage_rate_2018.htm.

8 Robin Goodwin, *Changing Relations: Achieving Intimacy in a Time of Social Transition* (Cambridge: Cambridge University Press, 2008); Maureen Baker and Vivienne Elizabeth, *Marriage in an Age of Cohabitation: How and When People Tie the Knot in the Twenty-First Century* (Ontario: Oxford University Press, 2014).

9 Linda J. Waite, Frances K. Goldscheider and Christina Witsberger, "Nonfamily Living and the Erosion of Traditional Family Orientations among Young Adults," *American Sociological Review* 51 (1986): 541–554.

10 Eric Klinenberg, *Going Solo: The Extraordinary Rise and Surprising Appeal of Living Alone* (New York: Penguin, 2012); Sue Heath, Katherine Davies, Gemma Edwards and Rachel M. Scicluna, *Shared Housing, Shared Lives: Everyday Experiences across the Lifecourse* (London: Routledge, 2019); Bella DePaulo, *Single with Attitude: Not Your Typical Take on Health and Happiness, Love and Money, Marriage and Friendship* (Scotts Valley, CA: Createspace Independent Publishing Platform, 2009); Sue Heath, "Young Adults and Household Formation in the 1990s," *British Journal of Sociology of Education* 4 (1999): 545–561.

11 Elizabeth Kenyon and Sue Heath, "Choosing This Life: Narratives of Choice among House Sharers," *Housing Studies* 16 (2001): 619–635; Annamarie Pluhar, *Sharing Housing: A Guidebook for Finding and Keeping Good Housemates* (East Dummerston, VT: Homemate Publishing, 2011).

12 Klinenberg, Going Solo; Sophia Maalsen, "I Cannot Afford to Live Alone in This City and I Enjoy the Company of Others: Why People Are Share Housing in Sydney,"

Australian Geographer 50, no. 3 (2019): 315–332; Oana Druta, Richard Ronald and Sue Heath, "Urban Singles and Shared Housing," Social and Cultural Geography 22, no. 9 (2021): 195–1203.

13 Sue Heath and Elizabeth Cleaver, *Young, Free and Single? Twenty-Somethings and Household Change* (Hampshire: Palgrave Macmillan, 2003); Kim McKee, Adriana Mihaela Soaita and Jennifer Hoolachan, "'Generation Rent' and the Emotions of Private Renting: Self-Worth, Status and Insecurity amongst Low-Income Renters," *Housing Studies* 35, no. 8 (2020): 1468–1487.

14 J. Wilson Mixon Jr. and E. Frank Stephenson, "Young and Out of Work: An Analysis of Teenage Summer Employment, 1972–2012," *Cato Journal* 36 (2016): 89–90; Sophie McNamara and John Connell, "Homeward Bound: Searching for Home in Inner City Share Houses," *Australian Geographer* 38 (2007): 71–91; Darrin Hodgetts, Kerry Chamberlain, Shiloh Groot and Yardena Tankel, "Urban Poverty, Structural Violence and Welfare Provision for 100 Families in Auckland," *Urban Studies* 51 (2014): 2036–2051.

15 Kay Saville-Smith and Bev James, *The Determinants of Tenure and Location Choices of 20–40-Year-Old Households in the Auckland Region* (Aotearoa: Centre for Housing Research, 2010).

16 Maureen McLaughlin, Tertiary Education Policy in New Zealand, 2003, www.fullbright.org.nz/voices/axford/mclaughlin.html; Richard Fry, "Young Adults, Student Debt and Economic Well-Being," *Pew Research Centre*, 2014, www.pewresearch.org/social-trends/2014/05/14/young-adults-student-debt-and-economic-well-being/; New Zealand Ministry of Education Student Loan Scheme Annual Report, December 2019, www.educationcounts.govt.nz/publications/80898/2555/student-loan-scheme-annual-report-2019.

17 Steffen Wetzstein, "The Global Urban Housing Affordability Crisis," *Urban Studies* 54, no. 14 (2017): 3159–3177.

18 Ministry of Business, Innovation and Employment, *Housing Affordability in New Zealand: Results* (Wellington, 2017), www.mbie.govt.nz/info-services/housing-property/sector-information-and-statistics/documents-and-images/-; Stats New Zealand, The State of Housing in Aotearoa New Zealand, December 15, 2020, www.stats.govt.nz/infographics/the-state-of-housing-in-aotearoa-new-zealand.

19 Joe Crawford and Kim McKee, "Hysteresis: Understanding the Housing Aspirations Gap," *Sociology* 52, no. 1 (2018): 182–197; Jennifer Hoolachan, Kim McKee, Tom Moore and A. M. Soaita, "'Generation Rent' and the Ability to 'Settle Down': Economic and Geographical Variation in Young People's Housing Transitions," *Journal of Youth Studies* 20 (2017): 63–78; Bob Day, "The Politics of Housing Affordability: A Contrived Crisis," *12th Annual Demographia International Housing Affordability Survey*, 2016, www.demographia.com/dhi.pdf.

20 Paul Schmelzer, "Increasing Employment Instability Among Young People? Labour Market Entries and Early Careers in Great Britain Since the 1980s," in *Young Workers, Globalisation and the Labour Market: Comparing Early Working Life in Eleven Countries*, eds Hans-Peter Blossfeld, Sandra Buchholz and Karin Kurz (Cheltenham: Edward Elgar, 2008), 181–206.

21 Heath, *Young Adults and Household Formation*; Charles Despres, *The Meaning and Experience of Shared Housing: Companionship, Security and a Home. Power by Design: Proceedings of the Twenty-Fourth Annual Conference of the Environmental Design Research Association* (Oklahoma City, OK: EDRA, 1994), 119–127.

22 Sue Heath, "Transforming Friendships: Are Housemates the New Family?," *Sociology Review* 14 (2004): 8–13; Jeffrey Weeks, Brian Heaphy and Catherine Donovan, *Same Sex Intimacies: Families of Choice and Other Life Experiments* (London: Routledge, 2001); Rachel M. Scicluna, *Home and Sexuality: The Other Side of the Kitchen* (London: Palgrave Macmillan, 2017).

23 Judith Stacey, *In the Name of the Family: Rethinking Family Values in the Postmodern Age* (Boston, MA: Beacon Press, 1996); Clare Thorpe, "Friends: The Show That

Changed Our Idea of Family," *Culture*, September 23, 2019, www.bbc.com/culture/story/20190920-friends-the-show-that-changed-our-idea-of-family.

24 Sophie McNamara and John Connell, "Homeward Bound."

25 Bella DePaulo, *How We Live Now: Redefining Home and Family in the 21st Century* (New York: Atria Books, 2015).

26 Heath et al., *Shared Housing*.

27 Scicluna, *Home and Sexuality*; De Paulo, *Single With Attitude*.

28 De Paulo, *How We Live Now*, 17.

29 Heath and Cleaver, *Young, Free and Single*; Anthony Giddens, *The Transformation of Intimacy: Sexuality, Love and Eroticism in Modern* Societies (Cambridge: Polity Press, 1992), 3.

3

CHOOSING FLATMATES

Stories abound about problematic flatmates with no shortage of damning indictments about sharing. Lazy, messy and dirty flatmates are a common gripe but there are also complaints about flatmates who never go out and sit in their bedrooms or watch TV all day; flatmates who steal or invite strangers into the house who steal housemates' belongings; flatmates who drink heavily; nocturnal flatmates; flatmates who are always late with or do not pay bills; flatmates who use everything fellow flatmates buy without invitation including food, toiletries and clothes.[1]

Unpleasant sharing experiences and stories of "flatmates from hell" are not unusual. Clearly, sharing domestic space can have its downsides but the negativity bias phenomenon suggests that people are more likely to pay attention to bad things that happen and give them more consideration than favourable events.[2] Concentrating on adverse accounts fails to recognise the beneficial aspects of sharing. Our research is consistent with previous findings in highlighting how sharing can be a largely positive experience.[3] For example, 25-year-old chef Max had this to say:

> *You know with about 97% of the people who moved through that place we all got along.*

While most things work well, for most people most of the time, potential difficulties underscore the importance of choosing viable flatmates, thereby hopefully avoiding problems.

Our initial research on house sharing investigated the unexamined area of selection or rejection of potential housemates.[4] The current social science literature is almost completely silent on this matter, and yet it's something that is extremely common as a practice among sharers. With this research focus, we hoped to address the simple question: What do people immersed in the flatting culture say about choosing prospective flatmates? In this way we hoped to explore more fully how sharers implement strategies to help avoid undesirable flatmates and add to the scant knowledge about this aspect of sharing.

DOI: 10.4324/9781003161370-3

In explanations and justifications for flatmate selection, it is clear that ideal flatmates are those who share many similarities with each other. This raises the question of discrimination since those different to oneself must, necessarily, be discriminated against. While freedom of choice over who we opt to live with is lawful in some countries, there are legal implications for discrimination in others. For example, in the USA rejected potential roommates have been awarded compensation for violation of discrimination laws. Consequently, John Messerly argued that given the intimacy and vulnerability of sharing accommodation prejudice in the choice of flatmates is a fundamental right. Subsequently, the 9th Circuit Court of Appeals has ruled that to prevent people from choosing housemates with compatible lifestyles is a serious invasion of privacy, autonomy and security.[5]

The New Zealand Human Rights Act (Sections 52–54) dealing with discrimination in the provision of land and housing prevents discrimination on the grounds of age, gender, race, religion, psychiatric illness, psychological impairment and sexual orientation.[6] The exception to this law is residential shared accommodation, which recognises the right to feel comfortable within the confines of domesticity. Nevertheless, such discrimination does contradict current social and political taboos against openly expressing prejudice. Consequently, participants were careful to pre-empt any suggestion of prejudice.

Finding flatmates

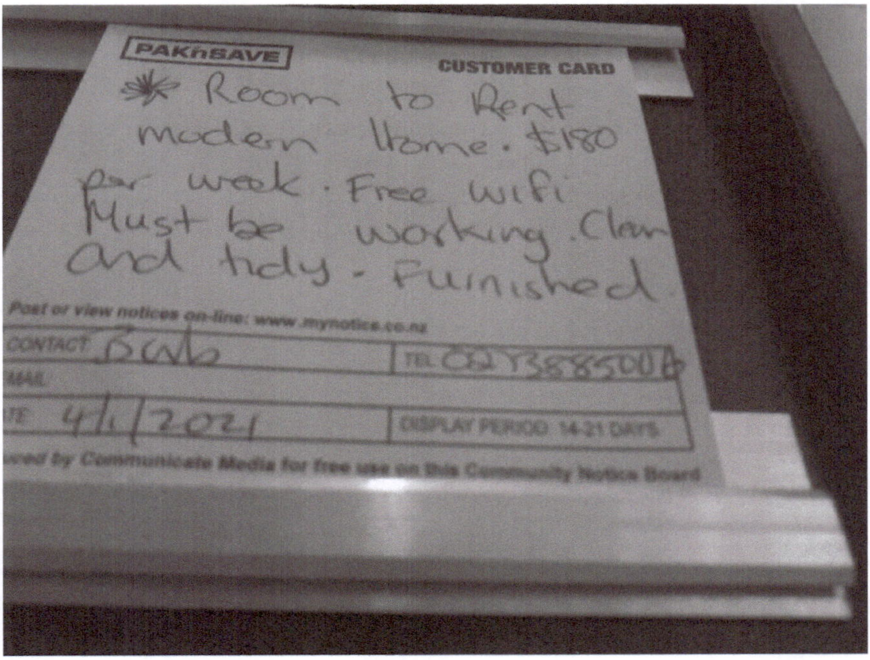

FIGURE 3.1 An example of a fairly typical advertisement in a supermarket.

Composing advertisements to appeal to the right potential flatmate can be vital. Not only is it necessary to make the household enticing but also a deterrent to those not wanted. The advertisement in Figure 3.1 does some serious business in terms of exclusions, and hence discrimination.

Where advertisements are placed is also important. Different places will reach different types of people. Individuals pursuing a healthy lifestyle will be better off advertising in a health shop rather than the local bar. Obviously, university notice boards will be more likely to attract students. More broadly, internet advertising, such as Facebook and Trademe, can reach well beyond the local supermarket.

The following is a Trademe advertisement. Not only is the home portrayed in a positive way but the ad also illustrates who or what might or might not be welcome in a potential flatmate.

> *UNFURNISHED bedroom available in a spacious home in . . ., nestled into a colourful and friendly little neighbourhood. The room has a built-in wardrobe and large windows that keep it bright and warm in winter, with black-out curtains for late mornings. The house has gas-heated water and a wood fireplace, making it easier and cheaper to keep comfortable and dry.*
>
> *This location is super convenient for someone working in town, 5 minutes' walk to a bus stop and less than 20 minutes' walk on flat ground into the city.*
>
> *Couples OK: No No Pets and Smokers:*
>
> *Ideal Flatmates:20–30 y/o working professional or post-grad student, preferably vegetarian, LGBT+ friendly.*

Apart from *LGBT+ friendly* this advertisement is fairly typical. While no advertisements include any suggestion of homophobia, this has a positive approach leaving no doubt for prospective applicants. Whereas much can be learned from browsing advertisements, our research examines what people say about their preferences and how these are explained and justified.

Once prospective housemates respond to an advertisement, interviews are conducted to assess suitability. Julie, a school counsellor in her mid-thirties, explains the interview process:

> *The way we go about it is we put an ad on trademe*
> *and then we get people that come round*
> *we want them to be kind of a lot like us*
> *so you have like 10 minutes to interview them*
> *to figure out whether they're your type of person or not . . .*
> *We just show them the room put them in the lounge*
> *introduce everybody, ask some general questions . . .*
> *One of the questions I always ask a person is*
> *do you have any hobbies*
> *because that tells me a lot about a person*

like if they are sporty you know they are going to get out there
they're an outgoing person or if they like computers
they're going to sit in their room
if they don't have any hobbies what do they do in their spare time
you can tell whether they are a social person or not
if they can make conversation

Much information is conveyed in this extract. The means of advertising is the internet. The choice of the interview is a physical meeting. The timing of the interview is 10 minutes. The strategy to assist assessment: sport and hobby questions are asked to evaluate sociability. Too much screen reliance or indoor activities are regarded as indicative of a lack of sociability and conversational skills. And finally, the need for similarity is expressed as "a lot like us". Sean, a recent postgraduate, stressed the importance of all current flatmates meeting possible housemates "face-to-face" after an online interview resulted in a "bad experience". In addition, if left solely up to a departing flatmate to find a replacement or sublet their room problems may arise as the person leaving may not have the same vested interest in finding the best candidate.

Rejection of an applicant does not necessarily imply that the person is not likeable but rather that the potential flatmate may jeopardise existing interpersonal dynamics. Temp worker Phoebe explains:

We did interview a couple of really lovely girls
you could just immediately see things that would
create tension potentially within the house
there was a woman who came
but we could tell that she had a very strong
personality and we got the feeling cause
Robyn is also quite a strong personality
I think we just knew that there could be
the potential for some conflict or stubbornness there
even though she was really nice

Selection of flatmates

Several common discourses emerged in the talk about selection criteria. Demographic and lifestyle factors considered in our discussion include age, gender, ethnicity, mental health, drug and alcohol use.

Age

A strong inclination for sharing with others of a similar age is pervasive. A quick scan of online advertisements for flatmates indicates a maximum of a ten-year age bracket consistent with our findings. The necessity for this was commonly attributed to age-related behavioural and socialising differences. Pat, a schoolteacher in her early thirties, explains why a similar age is preferable:

> *I wanted someone around the same age*
> *someone in their twenties* [or] *thirties*
> *because otherwise there would be*
> *too much difference in stage of life*
> *and it possibly wouldn't work out as well . . .*
> *I mean you want that person to feel comfortable in your house*
> *but at the same time you don't want to feel I can't do that*
> *because they have to have a quiet time*
> *you have to be able to live . . .*
> *I'm not going to not do things like having friends over or having a few drinks*
> *maybe a person who is older may not be into that kind of thing*

Presumed characteristics of older people objecting to friends coming round and having a few drinks or needing quiet time are used to explain age differences. The point is rightly made that everyone needs to feel comfortable and people need the freedom to live without unnecessary constraints. Conversely, much younger flatmates were also rejected as unacceptable. Mary, a library assistant and keen amateur dramatist in her early thirties, noted that she had matured since her very early twenties and was no longer a "party girl", while recently graduated Sean, an articulate 21-year-old, affirms that younger people like to party.

> *Obviously we're younger people in the flat*
> *we're aged between 19 and 21 years old*
> *so we enjoy parties catching up socially*
> *with alcohol and things like that . . .*
> *someone who just got to join in the flat*
> *needs to accept that there will be parties*

The narrow age range for this young group is important, suggesting that anyone older or not inclined to revelry might not be a good fit in the household, where parties are common occurrences. In addition, the need for sociability is highlighted. Sean also mentioned a widely held conviction that students and older professional people do not make compatible housemates. Very likely this conclusion is a result of a hard-earned experience that such household combinations can create tension. This is evident in Max's assessment of an unsuitable older flatmate:

> *There was a flatmate I had in the past that*
> *was really quite strict about her flat*
> *but the thing is she was sharing a flat with six other people*
> *all of us being young early twenties*
> *or still in university studying*
> *and she was a little bit older and*

just out of university and starting her own career
so it was really not the right
place for her to be in the first place
but she didn't appreciate the fact that
we were quite a rowdy bunch and everything

Max categorically states that the flat was not the "right place" for the more mature person given the noise levels. "Everything" could refer to a number of possibilities including partying and untidiness, which were mentioned by participants of more advanced age, who no longer enjoyed living in chaotic households. In addition, with the older woman having begun her career she was at a different stage of professional development than students, implying different paths and priorities.

School counsellor Julie mentioned that those working from 9 am to 5 pm require a good night's sleep in order to function effectively in the workplace. Keeping different hours and schedules can be, but not necessarily so, detrimental to flat harmony. The use of the word "professional" was ubiquitous. While the concept is multi-faceted, it also essentially addresses the necessity for full-time employment and economic self-sufficiency, as evident in Julie's talk.

We didn't want any couples or students
that's one thing we always put in our adverts
and like someone who's in the same age range who's a professional
someone that's working so that they can afford the rent

The point is clearly made that people without a steady income are less likely to be able to pay their bills. Rationally and justifiably, no one wants to flat out with someone who cannot meet their financial obligations. One graduate participant suggested that besides insufficient earning potential, an applicant's inability to understand the meaning of professional indicated a lack of intelligence indicating incompatibility. Clearly, "professional" does not include indigent students. Project manager Laura, in her late thirties, explains that students are less likely to have discretionary dollars for luxuries:

Mainly because of the age difference
but also because students have less money than we do
and we like to buy nice food and wine
and I guess students are less able to
participate in after work drinks and making dinners
and that kind of thing at night.

The more mature and professional lifestyle is defined by affordability and consumption of more expensive groceries, effectively excluding individuals who are young, unemployed and lacking qualifications. In England, Sue Heath and Elizabeth

Cleaver found that shared domestic arrangements beyond student years are popular among a relatively affluent section of the population, who gain qualifications. This trend is similar in Australia, where group households are represented at the high end of the income scale with a significantly less representation at the lower end.[7] This is endorsed by our research: not only is the ability to meet regular payments essential but an appreciation of the finer things in life is apparent. Clearly, even with working part-time, most students have little control over having sufficient funds for a decent lifestyle. This is in contrast to those who do not have, what one participant referred to as a "proper job". We understand this as non-student part-time workers. However, student status is temporary with the promise of a productive career.

Notably, students indicated a reciprocal aversion to sharing with older ages and professionals.

A common phrase employed in talk is "different life stages" with the expectation of distinct social and lifestyle activities from particular age groups. Age stood as a marker for a number of age-appropriate pursuits with late teens and early twenties more attuned to partying and those a decade older more focused on careers. In addition, the latter have more disposable income for more expensive aspects of consumption while those over 40 years are considered to need quiet time. Thus, age represents an important criterion for selection with age dissimilar others rejected on the grounds of difficulties fitting into an existing "flat dynamic". This is effectively protecting a lifestyle compatible with the interests and priorities of the existing flatmates. While age preference was inflexible, the criterion of gender was more flexible in its application.

Gender

The gender of potential flatmates appeared largely irrelevant with most stating unequivocally that it was not an issue. Talk of gender was centred on maintaining a gender balance within the household. If preferences were voiced, they were mostly biased towards women who were assumed to be better cleaners than men. Mid-twenties, sign writer Kelly delicately voices her view of differences between men and women:

> *Well not so much that they don't clean*
> *but their idea of cleaning is*
> *quite different to a female's perspective of cleaning*
> *and then there are a few other habits boys tend to have*
> *that girls don't have but no apart from that*
> *all the boys I have had have been cruisy*
> *easy to live with apart from one*

The gender stereotype assumes men fail to reach the standards set by women without acknowledging the possibility of fastidious male cleaners. Such seemingly insignificant statements endorse and perpetuate the perception that women are more suited to housework with the possible consequence that this will remain women's responsibility.[8] Kelly mentions other less endearing habits of men but fails to specify what they are. These criticisms are softened by asserting that, almost without exception, her male flatmates were easy to live with.

Gendered stereotypes are also reflected in teacher Pat's construction of a keen applicant as able to undertake traditional male domestic duties.

Ideally I wanted a female
but I wasn't worried either way
and he was really keen
and was obviously a person who would
do all the man jobs around the house
and I thought that would be cool
but for whatever reason it just didn't feel right

In further conversation, Pat revealed that while women are quite capable of lawn mowing she regarded this as a duty more suited to men. As such, an endorsement of traditional gender apportioning of labour. While there are positive aspects to having a man around to do male chores, and this is considered, ultimately the man is rejected not on gender grounds. Pat's decision is based on her need to feel comfortable about the person she lives with. Such reaction and intuition are important in considering with whom to share your domestic space. Earlier Pat had spoken of basing her decisions on "gut feeling" if she were unable to source references about applicants from people she knew. Whether the gut feeling is insight born of experience or intuitive social processing the male applicant is rejected. And this emphasises the power differential which favours the existing flatmates over the applicants.

All residents are expected to contribute equally to the running of the flat from chores to expenses. Traditionally gendered tasks are less likely. Frances Baum's 1986 study of gendered allocation of chores within shared accommodation suggested both traditional gender allocations of domestic chores and gender dexterity with men and women undertaking tasks typically associated with the other gender. In her study of household work allocation in all-male flats in Australia, Kirsten Natalier concluded that expectations of marriage may be institutionalised beyond wedlock and co-habitation into shared households.[9] However, both these studies are now decades old and exposure to non-genderised expectations of household chores could contribute to a decline in the convention operating within coupledom.

While stereotyping of genders was evident in the discussion of choice of flatmates, preference for specifically men or women was minimal beyond some seeking to find a balance of genders in a household. Julie explains that a balance is desirable and workable.

We try and keep an even balance
but if there is one person that comes in
that we like more than the other

it doesn't matter if they are male or female
we usually like to keep it balanced cause there's five of us
at the moment it's three boys and two girls
I mean I've had it when I've been the only girl
with four boys but we try to keep it sort of even
which works really well

Even if a gender-specific preference was stated, this is liable to be sabotaged by the most appealing applicant being chosen regardless of gender. Likeability trumps gender! Possibly, stress on a balance of genders can be understood in terms of recognition that there is less likely to be overt sexism or victimisation of a single flatmate of one gender. This was alluded to by Julie:

He was very disrespectful
it was hard for me cause I was the only girl among four boys
and I was the only one affected

The need for a gender balance was not elaborated beyond suggestions of vulnerability to mistreatment of a lone man or woman. Certainly, in an all-female flat interview, there were indications that a previous sole male occupant may have not been treated fairly and another where a lone female was clearly not considered on an equal footing with the males. Significantly, no one ascribed balance to different job distribution for males or females. Whereas gender was not regarded as important, ethnicity was talked about with considerable interactional caution.

Ethnicity

New Zealand is an ethnically varied society. In this section, we consider the prospect of sharing households with other nationalities, ethnicities or cultures. With regard to sharing with people of different ethnicities, three common discourses were identified: the necessity for enculturation; the importance of language and communication and acceptable behaviour. Failure to conform to any of these conditions justified rejection but was carefully presented as non-racist.

Sean speaks of living with a variety of different nationalities, who referred to their household as the United Nations flat.

You find that with people
who have been living in New Zealand
for the last six years which a lot had been
you only get this kind of small cultural quirks coming in
now and again

Sean suggests these flatmates have lived in New Zealand long enough to adapt to the accepted social mores and values. As such they are more likely to understand and comply with domestic expectations but norms may vary considerably from flat to flat. Cultural peculiarities are cast as trivial lapses, highlighting the importance of adopting host country norms. Enculturation is the necessary gradual assimilation by immigrants of appropriate cultural norms, practices and values of an adopted homeland.[10] With sufficient local experience and socialisation, cultural diversity is reduced to "small cultural quirks", which are unproblematic. Sean suggests six years is more than sufficient for acquiring cultural competency. Implicit in Sean's description is the ideological assumption that the values of the dominant local culture are "natural" compared to the cultural "quirks" of others.

A broad part of the culture of a country is the official language and an important criterion for new immigrants' adjustment and ability to fit in.[11] English is almost certainly the language spoken by most young adult sharers in New Zealand. Language is an important factor in considering prospective flatmates, as illustrated in the following by librarian Mary, who was looking for a flatmate at the time.

> *Asian girl and been in New Zealand since she was ten*
> *so no language barrier or anything*

A suitable length of time of residence in New Zealand for an applicant avoids potential problems with language and culturally different practices encapsulated by the vague "or anything". Project manager Laura gives a more detailed explanation of language barrier problems:

> *I've never chosen anyone who's been*
> *like* (an) *Asian exchange student*
> *mainly because of the fact that their*
> *English hasn't tended to be very good*
> *or indicated the type of person*
> *who spent a lot of time by themselves*
> *in their room or like up at university*
> *in the library or something like that*
> *and you know because we're*
> *a social flat I'd feel bad*
> *I feel it would be quite awkward*

While lack of English fluency is a standard basis for rejection, other ethnicities are also commonly categorised as being introverted and thus unable to fit in. This impacts the social dynamic of this flat and is considered unsuitable and awkward for both the household and the prospective flatmate. Failure to mention the possibility of exchange students who may be fluent in English demonstrates how subtle racism, however unintentional, persists.

The third ground for rejection is unacceptable behaviour. According to Martha Augoustinos and Danielle Every, out groups are negatively portrayed as violating social standards and these transgressions are often narrated in a storytelling format.[12] Rather than ethnicity, behaviour is the reason for rejection. This is apparent in Sean's account of problematic flatmates of different ethnicity.

> *They moved in and it didn't take us long to realise*
> *that they were quite peculiar*
> *one of them was actually royalty*
> *more or less his family was a couple of years ago*
> *and then it turns out that he's actually nocturnal*
> *he spends his entire day inside*
> *watching his DVD collection*
> *only coming out occasionally to*
> *breathe some air and cook himself some food*
> *so as far as flat dynamics, flat chores*
> *there wasn't much done*
> *and the other one was a controlling workaholic*
> *who would come back home and take it out on all of us*

Negative accounts suggest that previous bad experiences are often marshalled to justify the unsuitability of unwelcome applicants on the basis of violating behavioural norms rather than discrimination. Pragmatically, past adverse outcomes can be useful in avoiding the repetition of the same errors of judgement.

The extracts indicate that preferred flatmates are age-similar and gender-neutral with a cautious approach to ethnic difference. The answer to the question "who do you wish to share with?" is quite apparently "someone like myself". Similarity increases acceptability. A preference for similarity is, perhaps, not surprising given the intimacy involved in sharing and the considerable costs of making the wrong decision. At best, sharing can afford the social support of an informal family, which helps explain conservative decisions based on what we know and trust. Naturally, what we know and trust most are people like ourselves.

Rejection of potential flatmates is not bluntly about discrimination on the basis of age, gender or race but involves consideration of the right "fit" with existing flat dynamics. Possible threats to the harmony required for people to live successfully together are carefully policed and formulated as potential problems which might disrupt flat customs and practices. Similar pragmatics are adopted in considering potential flatmates with mental illness or addiction.

Mental health and substance use

Flatting inevitably entails close interpersonal interactions and minimal social distancing. In this section, we consider the willingness to live with someone who may have a mental illness or substance abuse problem. In discussing substance-related problems as separate from mental illness, we acknowledge the complexity of the debate over whether the former is best regarded as a disease, illness or lifestyle.[13]

This dispute is not likely to be resolved in the foreseeable future. Substance abuse can overlap with mental disorders with the two frequently co-morbid or co-occurring. However, treating addiction requires psychological understanding.

Mental health

Negative attitudes towards the mentally ill date back to ancient times and have been widely documented since the mid-twentieth century. In pioneering research, Shirley Star found that people regarded those with mental health problems as threatening, fearful and potentially dangerous and were thus averse to associating with them. Erving Goffman's seminal work on stigma and negative stereotyping endorsed these findings and identified reticence among those who had received treatment to disclose this. Tragically, negative public attitudes are as difficult to deal with as mental illness itself with internalised stigma and shame compounding symptoms. Goffman noted that stigma is essentially a shared social construction, a moral judgement of deviancy and disgrace that devalues individuals. Social rejection lies at the heart of stigma.[14]

Andrea Stier and Stephen Hinshaw argue that while open tolerance for most stigmatised groups has increased, stigma against mental illness persists.[15] The fear and perceptions of violence and volatility associated with mental disorders are believed to have grown in recent decades due to negative media portrayals, where the potential for violence is misattributed to a population whose majority is not dangerous.[16] More recent studies have demonstrated that increasing public understanding and tolerance of mental illness, driven by concerted campaigns to address stigma, has yet to result in better social acceptance.[17]

Common stereotyping of those with mental problems is that they are irresponsible, incompetent and unable to care for themselves. They are also believed to be able to control their illness and hence more responsible for their difficulties than people with physical illness, suggesting flawed character.[18] Finally, there exists a degree of benevolence towards the mentally ill where they are perceived as child-like and naïve. All these attributes were evident in talk of flatmate selection.

Participants referred to common problems, such as depression, and less specifically to creepiness, inappropriate behaviour or mental issues. These were closely associated with issues of safety, controllability or unemployment. Participants were often guarded in their responses when asked about mental illness suggesting an awareness of potential judgement by the researcher. Practical evaluation of others, based on past experience, was also evident in the talk about mental health and substance use and abuse. Julie speaks of a past flatmate who was asked to leave the household because of failed interpersonal relationships, attributed to a lack of respect.

> *I had one guy move in who turned out*
> *it didn't work out with him and me particularly*
> *like he would lie and was very disrespectful to me*
> *and in the end I had to ask him to leave*

I don't think he was all there
I didn't feel safe at one stage
you know he'd just do really creepy things
but when we had to interview him
I didn't necessarily like him but we had to find someone
and there was no one else so we had to take him
but ever since then we just make sure we don't
make a decision just to get someone in

"I don't think he was all there" suggests a psychological problem and this is further elaborated upon with the assertion of compromised safety due to creepiness. Lying is also associated with the flatmate's mental health. Julie's initial reservations about the prospective candidate were secondary to the economic necessity of finding someone to contribute to costs given the lack of other candidates. This unpleasant experience was a self-reflective lesson and deterrent to not take anyone in simply because of lack of available options. While Julie's response is quite vague, Laura speaks specifically mentioned depression.

I guess that would definitely be on a case by case basis
kind of situation so for example if it was somebody
who had depression I think you would struggle to find a flatmate
if you had a definite black mark beside someone who had depression
but I think if it would affect your ability to have social interaction
with that person if they had a mental illness
such that they couldn't function very well in a social situation
if they had a particularly bad case of say Asperger's or something similar
where their mental disability impacted their ability to function socially
then it would probably have to be on a case by case basis
you know in meeting them if it was something that really stood out strongly
as a negative factor then I would probably not want them to move in
but if it was something that didn't stand out at all or wasn't negative
then I think I would be okay with that

Acceptance is conditional. Mental health is assessed in terms of its impact on the ability to function in social situations. Social ineptness would almost certainly result in rejection as constraints around social interaction would be problematic for flatmates. Mental illness is tolerable provided it remains not overtly noticeable and without negative implications. This suggests acceptance of low-profile mental illness, such as depression, given its pervasiveness, provided it is subtle and remains effectively invisible.

Qualified tolerance is also evident in the next extract from Dom, a soldier in his late twenties.

If people were just up front about things that they had
like if they explained at the start that they may have some

mental issues and this is what I do and this is how I cope with it
or this is how you can help I would be more willing to consider it
but if it was like they didn't know how to control whatever issues they had
then that might influence me in a negative way

Dom would prefer future flatmates to be open about their illness and is willing to be of help. But for those with problems disclosing their condition can be a source of great anxiety given the significant discrimination they can face when their diagnosis is known to others. Dom also invokes the strict criterion that mental health problems should be well regulated, reinforcing the belief in the controllability of mental illness. Tolerance hinges on these unspecified mental health issues being controlled, minimally disruptive and effectively invisible.

In the next extract nursing student Kim talks about a former flatmate, whose problems are regarded as mental instability linked to stereotypical characteristics of irresponsibility, childishness, inappropriate behaviour and a potential threat to the safety of flatmates.

He couldn't take care of himself properly
so we tried to guide him as best we could
and I said to Mitchell you know we've just become parents to this boy . . .
We didn't really have time to nurture him the way he needed to be nurtured
so he would say inappropriate things
and do inappropriate things just to get attention from us . . .
So we played along but at other times it was just
downright annoying and rude [and] *inappropriate*
like he said some really inappropriate things to me . . .
I'm not comfortable with this guy in this place
especially when they have a mental instability
I mean he's a lot bigger than me
who knows what could have happened

Parenting suggests someone unable to care for himself and childlike in attention-seeking behaviour. Reactions to this behaviour are unfavourable. Although Kim leaves it up to the interviewer to come to her own conclusions as to "what could have happened", the size differential raises concerns for physical safety and earlier references to the flatmate's sexually explicit talk are suggestive of unpleasant possibilities. Odd behaviour as an assumed mental illness and potential for danger leads to rejection.

Based on past experience, Mary describes depression linked to unemployment.

In my experience those who have been between jobs
aren't very happy with their lives
I don't want to bring in someone who's depressed all the time
and really struggling with themselves
and bringing in a whole lot of emotional baggage
that is not to say that those who are working don't have issues as well

Emotional baggage is an interesting phrase, which carries with it the strong suggestion that such baggage is not to be tolerated. The inference is that depression negatively affects the social functioning of the flat and should be avoided. Although rejection is linked to depression associated with unemployment, the final sentence acknowledges that mental problems are not exclusive to the unemployed.

Stereotypical concepts are used in constructing those with mental problems as childlike, irresponsible, dangerous and unpredictable, thus justifying domestic distancing. This is evident in the stated difficulties of living with someone who needs care and support and resistance to "parenting" someone who should, ideally, be an equal participant in a shared household. Given the reciprocal and social nature of living with others, conditional acceptance is accorded to those with minor issues, which are unproblematic and manageable. The inability to control an illness is closely linked to fears of dangerousness and unpredictability. These combined with negative effects on the flat dynamic, past bad experiences and economic factors are used to explain what is acceptable and what is not.

Substance use

In comparison with mental disorders, substance-related disorders have a unique and universal stigma, are judged more harshly, and are regarded as self-inflicted and indicative of moral failure.[19] Tolerance for substance using co-residents is similar to criteria for acceptable housemates with mental health problems: the effect on the flat dynamic, responsibility, the degree of the problem and its invisibility.

Sean explains the negative aspects of living with someone who is "into" drugs with the recollection of an unpleasant experience involving a substance-abusing flatmate:

> *Over Christmas ended up going on an acid trip*
> *driving down to the beach and trying to collect*
> *all sorts of sacred elements and in the process half destroying our flat*

The danger and unpredictability associated with substance abuse and its destructive impact are apparent. This unpleasant experience informs Sean's present attitude towards potential substance-abusing flatmates.

> *We do enjoy parties catching up socially with alcohol*
> *and things like that although you know we've never really got into drugs*
> *or anything harder than alcohol itself . . . but at the same time*
> *you have to be careful not to get someone who actually is into drugs*
> *because that can open up a whole new can of worms*
> *and you know despite being students and stuff*
> *we are also quite conscientious people*

Partying is restricted to alcohol and is spoken of in terms of enjoyable socialising. Drugs are rejected with claims of conscientiousness of students with academic standards and performance required.

For most participants, acceptance of drug use was qualified by the proviso that drug taking should not be visible, as expressed by a school counsellor Julie.

If they want to do drugs
like if they want to smoke marijuana or whatever
we just say take it outside you know if they want to
put themselves in that situation they can
I haven't had flatmates like doing stuff blatantly in the open

Tolerance of drugs hinges on the distinction between inside and outside use. "Blatantly in the open" suggests the necessary furtiveness required for using soft drugs, bolstered by reference to flatmates putting themselves in "that situation", which could refer to issues of health, legality and addiction. Tolerance is thus subject to criteria of privacy, invisibility and responsibility. Paul, a graduate in his late twenties, working in the music media sector, has a similar opinion and explains that the household constitution forbids drug use, excluding marijuana. In a household of 22 people, a constitution would be necessary.

There're no drugs grown on the premises and I think the constitution says
that marijuana is the only drug that's allowed to be done
that said there's maybe only three people that smoke now
and its always outside and in their own private time and space

Clearly, marijuana is acceptable provided that use is not blatant and jeopardising secure accommodation for flatmates. According to librarian Mary, party drugs are also tolerable provided use is infrequent.

I don't want to live with someone who's taking lots of drugs
I mean we smoked a bit of pot at uni but nothing since then
and certainly wouldn't want to be living with
someone who used drugs regularly
I mean a lot of my friends will still go to concerts
and they might take a pill for a dance gig
but no one who is taking drugs on a daily or weekly basis
yeah not my kind of thing and often there's
just trouble that comes along with them
and their friends often turn out to be a bit dodgy

Mary attributes cannabis use as the sort of thing students do. An acceptable norm of recreational drugs is constructed in terms of "what", "where" and "when". Pills (soft drugs) at dance gigs (social gatherings) are permissible but regular and frequent use is not. Trouble in the past with regular drug users is implied but not elaborated on. "Dodgy" was a common adjective used by participants for describing regular drug users. The term is not specific but has connotations of unreliable, dishonest, unlawful and risky characteristics.

For project manager Laura, recreational drug use, as opposed to addiction, is driven by economic responsibility and the social impact on the flat.

> *I take drugs recreationally like not all the time*
> *but you know I have done in the past*
> *I mean I'm not opposed to people who use drugs*
> *in saying that I wouldn't want to live with an addict*
> *or someone who used drugs very very frequently*
> *but in terms of people who take drugs that's okay*
> *as long as it doesn't impact on their*
> *ability to pay rent* [and] *their ability to pay bills*
> *and after work to have a nice meal*
> *and a glass of wine in a social kind of way . . .*
> *A question I would be more likely to ask people*
> *who were thinking of moving here*
> *is how they felt about drug use*
> *I wouldn't like to light up a joint*
> *and have them completely freak out*

Laura's talk highlights the socialising aspect of alcohol and recreational substance use where a distinction is made from the problems associated with abuse. Acceptability is determined by social context and frequency of consumption.

Substance use and abuse are complicated by the positive social associations with psychoactive substances. Drinking alcohol is legal and very much part of most Western cultures, lubricating social interaction and being associated with good times. In some youth cultures the use of illicit drugs, such as dance drugs and cannabis, is common. Social acceptance and normalisation of sensible recreational drug use, even by abstaining young adults, have been documented in the UK, with cannabis being the most tolerated.[20] In the past decade, cannabis has become increasingly decriminalised and legalised for both medicinal and recreational use.

Psychoactive qualities make substance use both attractive and threatening, with both positive and negative values. Alcohol is interesting in that consumption is almost essential in some flats, where partying is part of the flat culture. There are limits as well as important distinctions between social drinking and recreational soft drug use and chronic hard use. Negative connotations are associated with addiction with boundaries to what is tolerable by otherwise law-conforming householders, seemingly aware of the problematic health, legal ramifications and deviance associated with excessive drug use and the wider drug culture. Dangerousness and unpredictability are allied with both chemical dependency and mental illness. Rejection is thus based on the need to be safe and trusting of those one shares with.

There is qualified acceptance of substance users who act with discretion and responsibility and pose no threat to foundational aspects of the flat, particularly with respect to economic viability and legality. Substance abuse is not condoned and invokes the stigma, distancing and exclusion related to mental disorders. Similarly, mental illness is not straightforward in terms of acceptance or rejection, with notable comments about the pervasiveness and acceptability of some problems, such as depression. Mental illness that is controlled or effectively invisible is not subject to rejection. The overriding theme is that flatmates should be "people like me", implying economic, social and psychological reciprocity, contributing to flat life rather than being a drain on the flat dynamic.

Selecting a new member of the flat is to replace someone who has left. People move for various reasons besides being asked to leave, they change jobs, travel to other countries, move cities or take up residence with a partner. This highlights the transitory nature of shared living.

Conclusion

Finding the right flatmate requires discrimination if shared living is to function effectively. Potential problems in flatmate choice must be astutely assessed as mistakes can be costly. Preferred flatmates are those similar in age and ethnicity with gender less important. Clearly, substance abusers and the mentally ill are not preferred people to live with. Nevertheless, the luxury of finding the best person to share with can be sabotaged simply by economic necessity and the need to fill an empty room as soon as possible to avoid additional rent costs. This also highlights the transitory nature of shared living. In the following chapter, we examine how desirable flatmates are constructed and how young adults actively seek to avoid potentially complicating household relationships.

Notes

1 For example, Eric Klinenberg, *Going Solo: The Extraordinary Rise and Surprising Appeal of Living Alone* (New York: Penguin, 2012).

2 Roy F. Baumeister, Ellen Bratslavsky, Catrin Finkenauer and Kathleen D. Vohs, "Bad Is Stronger Than Good," *Review of General Psychology* 5, no. 4 (2001): 323–370.

3 Sue Heath and Elizabeth Cleaver, *Young, Free and Single? Twenty-Somethings and Household Change* (Hampshire: Palgrave Macmillan, 2003).

4 This chapter draws on work published by the authors in two journals: Vicky Clark and Keith Tuffin, "Choosing Housemates and Justifying Age, Gender and Ethnic Discrimination," *Australian Journal of Psychology* 67 (2015): 20–28. Copyright ©Australian Psychological Society, reprinted by permission of Taylor & Francis Ltd, www.tandfonline.com on behalf of Australian Psychological Society; Keith Tuffin and Vicky Clark, "Discrimination and Potential Housemates with Mental or Substance Abuse Problems," *Journal of Language and Social Psychology* 35 (2016): 98–118.

5 John T. Messerly, "Roommate Wanted: The Right to Choice in Shared Living," *Iowa Law Review* 93 (2008): 1949–1980; Terry Baynes, "Roommate-Matching Site Does Not Violate Housing Laws," *U.S. News*, February 3, 2012, www.reuters.com/article/us-roommates-lawsuit-idUSTRE8112JP20120202.

6 New Zealand Legislation, *Human Rights Act 1993, Public Act No. 82 (section 53 & 54)* (Wellington: Parliamentary Counsel Office, 2017), www.legislation.govt.nz/act/public/1993/0082/13.0/DLM304212.html.

7 Heath and Cleaver, *Young, Free and Single*; Sophie McNamara and John Connell, "Homeward Bound: Searching for Home in Inner Sydney's Share Houses," *Australian Geographer* 38 (2007): 71–91.

8 Ellen Berscheid, "Forward," in *The Psychology of Gender*, eds Anne E. Beall and Robert J. Sternberg (New York: Guildford Press, 1993), vii–xvii.

9 Frances Baum, "Shared Housing: Making Alternative Lifestyles Work," *Australian Journal of Social Issues* 24 (1986): 197–212; Kristen Natalier, "'I'm Not His Wife': Doing Gender in Share Households," Unpublished Doctoral Thesis. University of Queensland, 2003.

10 Rose Capdevila and Jane E. M. Callaghan, "'It's Not Racist. It's Common Sense,'" *Journal of Community and Applied Social Psychology* 18 (2008): 1–16.

11 Antonia C. Lyons, Helen Madden, Kerry Chamberlain and Stuart Carr, "'It's Not Really Discriminating Against Immigrants It's More Telling People How to Fit in': Constructing the Nation in Immigration Talk in New Zealand," *Journal of Community and Applied Social Psychology* 21 (2011): 14–27.

12 Martha Augoustinos and Danielle Every, "The Language of Race and Prejudice: A Discourse of Denial, Reason and Liberal Practical Politics," *Journal of Language and Social Psychology* 26 (2007): 123–142.

13 Edmund Hendenl, Hans Olav Melberg and Ole Jørgen Røgeberg, "Addiction: Choice or Compulsion?," *Frontiers in Psychiatry*, no. 4 (August 7, 2013): 77. https://doi.org/10.3389/fpsyt.2013.00077.

14 Wulf Rössler, "The Stigma of Mental Disorders: A Millennia-Long History of Social Exclusion and Prejudices," *EMBO Reports* 17, no. 6 (2016): 1250–1253; Shirley A. Star, "The Public's Ideas About Mental Illness." Paper Presented at Annual Meeting of the National Association for Mental Health, Indianapolis, IN, November 1955; Erving Goffman, *Stigma: Notes on the Management of Spoiled Identity* (Englewood Cliffs, NJ: Prentice Hall, 1963).

15 Andrea Stier and Stephen P. Hinshaw, "Explicit and Implicit Stigma Against Individuals With Mental Illness," *Australian Psychologist* 42 (2007): 106–117.

16 Otto Wahl, *Media Madness Public Images of Mental Illness* (New Brunswick, NJ: Rutgers University Press, 1995).

17 For example, Georg Schomerus, Herbert Matschinger and Matthias C. Angermeyer, "Causal Beliefs of the Public and Social Acceptance of Persons With Mental Illness: A Comparative Analysis of Schizophrenia, Depression and Alcohol Dependence," *Psychological Medicine* 44, no. 2 (2014): 303–314.

18 Otto F. Wahl, *Media Madness*.

19 Bruce G. Link, Jo C. Phelan, Michaeline Bresnahan, Ann Steuve and Bernice A. Pescosolido, "Public Conceptions of Mental Illness: Labels, Causes, Dangerousness, and Social Distance," *American Journal of Public Health* 89 (1999): 1328–1333.

20 Howard Parker, Lisa Williams and Judith Aldridge, "The Normalisation of Sensible Recreational Drug Use. Further Evidence for the North-West England Longitudinal Study," *Sociology* 36 (2002): 941–964.

4

DESIRABLE FLATMATES

Having considered the formation of households and issues impacting the selection of housemates, we will now examine the attributes of "desirable" flatmates. Of course, there is a strong link between who is selected to join a flat and the ideal person(s) to live with. The shared housing literature abounds with examples showing how things can go terribly wrong and it's safe to assume that people seek to avoid negative situations if possible. This chapter seeks to shed light on what people say about housemate desirability and successful co-residence. Additional overlays, which invariably arose, were around the issues of living with friends or strangers and whether couples or singles are preferred.[1] As the data will illustrate, preferences and ideals are based on past experiences of what worked and what failed to work.

Living together presents its own unique challenges with a growing plethora of anecdotal advice on how to be a good housemate. This ranges from avoiding strong perfume and lengthy reading on the toilet to equal sharing of unpopular chores. Experienced sharers are acutely aware of and seek to avoid potential problems, which may destabilise the domestic environment. Four dominant discourses surfaced in the talk about desirable housemates: interpersonal similarity; common expectations; the importance of trust and comfort; and the need to be simultaneously independent and sufficiently sociable.

Interpersonal similarity

In this key discourse, the importance of flatmates sharing various similarities, such as interests, values and lifestyles, is stressed. As in flatmate selection, being within the same age range is also central to the similarity discourse. A married couple, Mike and Susie, still sharing with one housemate, ascribe a past functional flat to

DOI: 10.4324/9781003161370-4

having the same interests and upbringing. They reflect on differences that could make flat relationships difficult:

Susie: *All kind of had the same upbringing*
Mike: *We had a lot of the same interests*
Susie: *And I think it would be hard*
if someone was completely foreign or something
Mike: *Or completely opposite*
Susie: *In values . . .*
Mike: *We didn't want vegetarians*
we were pretty selective like that
it sounds bad but us like
we're all hunters and gatherers
and everyone just couldn't be bothered
with cooking separately

Similarity in upbringing, interests and values are regarded as promoting compatibility. Disparities in values, cultural differences and contrasting lifestyle choices are suggested as negative, problematic and detrimental to domestic harmony. Ideological differences between vegetarians and hunters are compounded by the practical aspect of having to cook separately. Mike and Susie flat is in a large New Zealand town, where flatmates tend to cook and eat together: city-shared householders were found to be more likely to prepare meals on an individual basis.

Consistent with preferences for potential flatmates in the same age bracket, compatibility is considered to be fostered by parallel life stages. Lucy, an extremely experienced flatter, cites age difference as one reason why a younger flatmate did not fit in.

He was just a boy in a different space
we had asked when we were looking for people
for folks in their thirties
and who had done a bit of travel
that was on our ad and when he came
he said that was his experience
and then after he had been in the house
for about two or three weeks he said,
"Actually I'm not in my thirties
and haven't done that much travel,"
and he was like ten years younger than us
and it was like that's obvious
wow there's a reason why we want those things
because we're not in the same space

Age, represented abstractly as "space", is a code for other factors such as experience, worldliness and a cosmopolitan lifestyle. Differences in lifestyle, linked to age and experience, underscore the importance of similarity and levels of tolerance. Postgraduate Pia speaks of no longer being accepting of some behaviour often associated with student flats.

I'm just so over that at the moment
I don't want to live with gross people
who're drinking every weekend
and absolutely wasted
and the house is a mess
because they don't know how to tidy up
and things like that

A distinct progression from undergraduate revelry and somewhat insalubrious conditions to a more sedate and comfortable lifestyle is evident in many talks, for example, the discretionary dollars to accommodate a more sophisticated palate than student food. "And things like that" is non-specific, suggesting that untidiness and partying are but two examples from a wider list of youth-oriented behaviour that Pia is no longer willing to tolerate.

As stated by student Jody, corresponding lifestyles and leisure activities are believed to reduce possible conflict and promote socialising.

So either like the same type of movies or maybe TV shows
so that's something you can do together
it kind of helps if you've the same lifestyle
so if your boy friends are staying up till 11 o'clock at night
watching TV shows or whatever
cause I found in past flats
when you do have different lifestyles
that's when there's more conflict

Watching TV shows or movies together increases the social glue of the flat, while different tastes make it difficult or impossible to agree on entertainment, diminishing the scope for something to do together. This underscores the importance of group sociability rather than one-on-one relationships among flatmates. Keeping different hours was touched on frequently, with varying degrees of importance. On average similar sleeping patterns are preferred, especially by those working from 8 am to 5 pm. This is likely to relate to the need for quiet sleeping environments for those having to arise early in the morning for work. The stated importance of similarities in entertainment choices and bedtimes is related to a reduction in conflict, while differences can contribute to friction.

Overwhelming consensus is for living with people who are very similar. Differences are less easy to relate to and can be detrimental to household viability. The proverb "birds of a feather flock together" succinctly describes this discourse. Differences go beyond simple grounds for exclusion. Similar ages, backgrounds, interests, values and morals are regarded as essential in ensuring the wheels of co-existence are well greased. Similarities promote bonds: too many differences can lead to disengagement. Those who share similar backgrounds and values most effectively provide reciprocal connectedness and social support. Closely aligned to the necessity for personal similarities is the importance of parallel expectations of what is considered appropriate or improper behaviour within the flat.

Common expectations

Harmony is easier to achieve if flatmates have corresponding expectations of each other. Maree is a project manager in her early thirties:

> *I guess good communication*
> *in terms of expectations around what you want*
> *to do in terms of chores, entertainment or friends*
> *just having a common understanding*
> *of what's okay and what's not?*

Effective communication is essential for navigating expectations of what is acceptable in a household or not. In an otherwise unregulated environment, similarities and commonality of expectations are all important. As discussed in more detail in Chapter 5, equal sharing of chores can be a particular bone of contention. Housemates having similar expectations of each other is important for functional, enjoyable flatting. This acknowledges that people have different ideas about house sharing, such as the amount of socialising required; similar perspectives on cleanliness and tidiness; security; heating in communal areas; having friends to stay and purchasing of consumables. Since unmet expectations can result in resentment they need to be realistic and flexible. For example, conflict is bound to arise if a meticulous flatmate dictates that the flat should be immaculate at all times. Entertainment and friends are discussed both positively and negatively. Having friends for dinner, with everyone involved, is spoken of with enjoyment. Inviting strangers to impromptu parties is regarded as putting the flat and possessions at unnecessary risk and presumably defying common expectations. Quite obviously, there are numerous issues where problems can arise and where shared expectations are important to avoid conflict and misunderstanding.

A common expectation is that shared housing is a "home" rather than merely a roof overhead. Flatmates who only want a room to rent contravene the need to be suitably sociable. Lucy enlarges on this:

> *It's having the same expectations about flatting*
> *or what it means to live in the same house*
> *and for the most part for me home . . .*
> *we just had different expectations about*

what living in this house was
I wanted a home, he just wanted a cheap room
I don't want someone just to fill a room
because I have to live and share sometimes
a small space with this person
I want to be comfortable being myself in my home
and I want the other person to be comfortable too
when I was living in London I looked at a house
that was a big beautiful old place
and every room had a padlock on every door
and I was, "There's no way I'm living here,"
it was about renting a room . . .
and then there's a shared kitchen
I think there was a roster for the shower
Otherwise, "Hi I don't know who you are in the hallway
but, hi there," back to my room

Sharing a home rather than renting a room presupposes regular, congenial social interaction, rather than brief encounters in passages or kitchens. Sue Heath and Elizabeth Cleaver distinguish between two different types of share-houses: those characterised by friendships and those where residents do not know each other or share leisure time together at home.[2] A random collection of people who have a room in a house defies the notion of "home". Such anonymous households were briefly acknowledged by our participants but generally associated with flatting outside of Australasia. Unfavourable comparisons were made with those where in-house socialising is expected, provided independence and privacy are not compromised. Reciprocal comfort of all flatmates was often stressed. People are far more likely to feel comfortable and trust others similar to themselves and these interconnected requirements form the basis of the third discourse relating to desirable flatmates.

Comfort and trust

A common aspect threaded through this discourse is the rational need to feel comfortable and secure in one's own home. Maree draws on the similarities discourse as contributing to comfortable relationships.

You might also have the same
everything, like political views or
taste in food and that sort of thing
because all of these things, I think, if they're not there
then those relationships can be that little harder
to just be comfortable around people
in such close quarters

Relationships when living in close domesticity are more difficult to sustain if there are differences. Too many disparities can result in discomfort and tension with the degree of comfort closely tied to the degree of similarity. "That little harder" is a nice understatement of the importance of similarity within the intimacy of shared living.

Lucy speaks of a flatmate making communal areas uncomfortable spaces.

And it just didn't work
it felt uncomfortable coming in here
didn't feel like it was my own space
and Dave had the same experience and
because he was a bit socially awkward
and not respectful of conversations we were having
and kind of just unaware

The flatmate was asked to leave shortly after moving in. The interview with policy analyst Lucy was conducted in the flat communal lounge, hence the reference to "in here". The choice of the words "my own space" stresses the need for communal areas to be enjoyed by all but also implies an unacceptable degree of discomfort attributed to the presence of the unsuitable flatmate. This assertion is validated through an external source, a fellow flatmate Dave. "Unaware" suggests a lack of sensitivity to others. Sensitivity, consideration and respect have been identified as contributing to successful co-residence. A basic prerequisite for feeling comfortable with others is trust.

Trust in shared housing extends to many areas, including feeling safe at home and relying on flatmates to adequately secure the premises. Policeman Mike spoke of the paramount importance of trust.

I think you just need to be able to trust them
that's probably one of the other biggest things
that you need is to be able to trust someone
[if not] *then you wouldn't be able to live together*

The pivotal role of trust is clearly evident in the use of the maximiser "biggest" with living together deemed impossible if trust is lacking. Thirty-five-year-old Lisa, a call centre worker, spoke of the growing wariness of flatmates who could not be trusted, which ultimately led to her leaving the household.

You couldn't trust to leave money lying around because it got taken

This was not merely a case of carelessly leaving money around, tempting theft, but regular pilfering from the communal kitty, necessary to fund common consumer items, such as toilet paper or sugar. Such dishonesty breeds distrust and distress. Of all the interviews, Lisa's experience of a dysfunctional household stood out as very different to other accounts of essentially positive experiences of sharing.

Housemates need to be trusted when it comes to household security. In the following extract Phoebe, a temp worker in her late twenties, talks of a careless flatmate, whose lack of experience in flatting made the household vulnerable. Phoebe attributed this deficit to taking on a flatmate straight from her family home.

Yesterday she left her windows wide open
she had left a big gap
enough for someone to crawl through
and left her bedroom door open
it was freezing and it had started raining
and I was like I know I probably
shouldn't go into her room
but I need to leave the house soon
and I'm not going to leave the window wide open
for security reasons and cold

By entering a housemate's room uninvited, to secure the premises, Phoebe acknowledges and verifies the general rule of bedrooms being off limits to other flatmates. Trust assumes that flatmates will respect personal and private boundaries. Ideally setting and defending boundaries should not be necessary but dealing with breaches sometimes becomes unavoidable, as Lisa found with a flatmate overstepping boundaries.

I thought enough is enough
you walk in, now I know that we are friends
but you are crossing boundaries
by now thinking you are allowed to
randomly walk into everybody's room
so I knocked that on the head
I kept my door closed after that
if he knocked I'd answer it
but I had to nip it in the bud
and Helen started locking her door

Sue Heath notes that in the intimacy of shared households there is a blur between the usual Western demarcation of public and private spaces.[3] Homes are places where non-family members are usually invited guests, who seldom venture beyond lounge, dining and bathroom areas. Our research demonstrates that bedrooms in shared housing are almost exclusively individual zones of privacy and autonomy. Friendship between flatmates is seldom a permit to free run of bedrooms. Privacy is an expectation, rather than a personal preference. Knocking before entering bedrooms is indicative of sacrosanct boundaries. Intolerable intrusion needs to be promptly dealt with to prevent the escalation of unacceptable behaviour. Breaching boundaries within the flat compromises fundamental comfort and trust, essential in sharing with others. The need to lock a bedroom indicates a serious breakdown in the trust expected from those one shares with and the degree to which trust has been compromised. As Lucy explained earlier, locked doors do not make a home. Julie's account of a flatmate overstepping boundaries is more ominous:

> *I heard him come home really drunk*
> *and then I sort of went back to sleep*
> *and then he was like,*
> *"Ah did you did you hear me*
> *coming into your room last night?"*
> *it was me and all boys*
> *and I just said to the other guys*
> *because I'd been living there for quite a while*
> *I just said, "He's got to go*
> *I don't feel comfortable" . . .*
> *he's the one I had to ask to leave*

Uninvited intrusion into bedrooms can signify serious offence and a risk to personal privacy and safety with negative psychological consequences. The implications of the flatmate's intent are suggestive, leaving Julie feeling extremely uncomfortable. This is very similar to Kim's (Chapter 3) account of unpleasant, sexually suggestive talk of a flatmate making her feel uneasy. Earlier Julie had referred to the flatmate as "creepy". "He's got to go" has the same potency as Lisa's "enough is enough". Both these flatmates irretrievably crossed a threshold. The negative psychological stress brought on by such episodes is clear: intrusion into a flatmate's private space is taboo, highlighting the importance of trust, personal security and safety in shared domesticity. In this case, the flatmate was asked to leave following a breach of one of the basic rules of sharing.

We take for granted that homes are stable places of security, regeneration and rest. To not feel at ease in one's own home may result in physical and psychological stress.[4] In keeping with this expectation, participants spoke of their homes as sanctuaries with a need to feel comfortable and safe in both communal and private areas. Integral to feeling comfortable, in such an intimate domestic setting, is trust. Given the close proximity of people in shared living, the greater the trust, the more comfortable and successful interpersonal relationships are likely to be.

Sue Heath and Elizabeth Cleaver found that undesirable flatmates are frequently those who breach physical and symbolic boundaries and our findings endorse this.[5] Such transgressions compromise fundamental trust which must be maintained if the flat is to remain a place of safety, relaxation and freedom from threats to security and well-being. A related but more subtle and nuanced aspect of desirable flatmates is the importance of a critical balance between independence and social connection without compromising physical and psychological boundaries.

Balancing independence and social connection

Independence and privacy are highly valued in Western cultures.[6] Seemingly paradoxical is the pervasive importance research participants placed on privacy and independence together with a strong desire for human connection. In particular, they stressed the need for sociability among flatmates and the potential for friendship. The ability to astutely manage tensions between both independent and socially connected lives is regarded as essential to successful household relationships.

Librarian Mary articulates the enjoyment of both connection and independence.

> *We got on like a house on fire*
> *it was great but it was lovely too*
> *to have our own space*
> *on his days off we spent a lot of time together*
> *we shared the same tastes in many things*
> *and we're still good friends*

Socialising includes doing things together, cementing flat cohesion and enjoying connectedness. Emphasis is placed on friendship, which extended beyond the period they shared a house together. There were many references by participants to enduring friendships lasting well beyond sharing the same roof overhead. Expression of the enjoyment of social interaction is invariably countered by the necessity for "space", which we interpret as incorporating both territorial (bedroom) and psychological space. Intrusiveness has the opposite effect. Failure to appreciate the crucial nature of privacy violates rights, leading to discord in relationships.[7] Annie, a midwife in her mid-twenties, enlarges on the complex nuances of the requirement.

> *I think it's important to know*
> *when people need their space as well*
> *even though you're living together*
> *and you're friends doesn't mean you need to*
> *be in each other's face all the time*
> *Claire definitely likes to have her own space*
> (Claire: *I can be a bit of a hermit crab*)
> *so after work I'll be less likely to go talk to her*
> *not because I don't want to but because I know that*
> *she will come out when she's ready*

Annie stresses the importance of being aware of flatmates' differing needs for connection and how she deals with the situation, indicating a respectful sensitivity to her flatmate's needs. "In each other's face all the time" suggests being suffocatingly close and disregard for need of privacy.

People differ in their individual needs for socialising but this requirement can also change from time to time. A subtle sensitivity to the emotional states of housemates and respecting private time are important for success or failure in domestic relationships. Phoebe, in her late twenties, speaks of going through a bad patch with little understanding from a flatmate.

I was just wanting to hole myself up
in my bedroom and just read books
and watch films and stuff for a few weeks
and she commented on it
and made it into quite a big deal
she though it was affecting her
I think some people are
that much more sensitive to
things like that or expect to be best friends
with you if you are living together
or some people don't try at all and think
you should lead separate lives and so I think
it's striking the balance between sociable
you know friendly but also independent

Domestic intimacy does not necessarily equate with psychological and emotional intimacy. Phoebe raises the matter of the differing degrees of closeness expected in sharing, from close friendship to separate lives. Both Frances Baum and Sue Heath found that different assumptions about socialising expected from housemates can undermine relationships.[8] Independence needs to be weighed against sociability. This dichotomy lies at the heart of the discourse of independent but connected. Phoebe concludes that striking a balance between the two is the ideal resolution.

According to the privacy regulation framework, individuals actively seek out either social contact or solitude, depending upon their immediate inclinations.[9] Sensitivity to fluctuating emotional states, such as the quiet period needed by Phoebe, without the stimulation of others is beneficial for some. This maintains both the collective harmony of the flat and that of the individuals who make up the household. Interpersonal sensitivity to these nuances is noted by Owen, a resident in an all-male student flat.

We can read each other's moods quite well
which helps us avoid conflict
if one of us is in a bad mood
then it's really easy for us
to just not bother them

Being aware of a flatmate's mental state is important in assessing how sociable or independent a person is likely to be at a given time. In this example, a bad mood leads to the decision to temporarily suspend assumptions of sociability. These subtleties demonstrate the complex dynamic of interpersonal relationships and the importance of being able to read the moods of those who make up the collective.[10]

Sue Heath and colleagues found similar requirements for careful management of interpersonal relationships: the balance required between communality and privacy and negotiating of connections and disconnections. They differentiate between getting on (those who maximise shared time and build meaningful relationships and collective identities) and getting through (those who minimise domestic socialising).[11] Private time and space are valuable for security, control and identity expression through arrangement of personal possessions while shared time and space build quality relationships.

Central to the discourse of separate but connected is the Western ideology of individualism, independence and right to privacy. Private space in the Western world is regarded as essential for well-being, while in collective cultures the greater good of the group overrides individual rights and desires. Optimally, shared households need to incorporate both collectivism and individualism for functional co-residence.[12] A balance between the ideals of both provides a critical basis for a workable shared household and maintaining relationships. Friendship among flatmates is highly valued and assumes reciprocal trust. The same cannot be assumed of strangers. Is it preferable to share a household with friends or strangers?

Avoiding complications in relationships

This section also considers who might be considered a desirable housemate but centres around pre-existing relationships among and between flatmates. Is it better to flat with friends or strangers, couples or single individuals? The necessity for considering these additional aspects, which can sustain or undermine successful co-residence, accentuates the complex permutations of interpersonal relationships in the intimacy of domestic settings. Living with friends or strangers will undoubtedly have different effects on flat dynamics.

Friends versus randoms

While the appeal of setting up a home with friends is understandable, why do some opt to flat with unknown people? Sharing with friends, or at least known acquaintances, requires less uncertainty, and therefore, potentially less risk. However, sharing with unknown people carries the possibility of these flatmates becoming friends. For young adults these decisions are never straightforward but we do know that undergraduates typically move in with friends they have met in their first year of study, as sharing with strangers can be a source of anxiety.[13] Julie speaks of the apprehension of moving in with unknown people.

> *I was really scared when I went*
> *flatting with randoms*

I only used to flat with people I knew
and then when I started doing it
I thought to myself if this
doesn't work out I can just move out

"Randoms" is commonly used to describe flatmates who are initially unfamiliar but can also refer to flatmates who do not belong to an inner core of flatmates. A "random" individual may be brought into a flat with a group of friends for purely financial reasons. This destabilises the assumption of equality and democracy in shared households with the potential for marginalisation. Anxiety about flatting with unknown people was often accompanied by assurance that flatting affords the opportunity to move out if a situation becomes unbearable, again underscoring the transitory nature of flatting.

Town-based saleslady Donna, living in an all-women flat, advocates living with friends.

With friends it's not complete strangers
so you don't have to be awkward

Living with friends can preclude initial unease or fear of living with the unknown, stemming from suddenly sharing a kitchen, bathroom and living spaces with someone who yesterday was a complete stranger. This can be anxiety-provoking for some and can be avoided by electing to share with known people. Two builders in their late twenties, living in the same town as Donna, were similarly in favour of flatting with friends.

Ben: I've been pretty lucky with flatmates, all been mates
Jeff: Yeah over here you don't really move in
with anyone you don't know
especially in (town name)
it's such a small place

Being lucky with flatmates was frequently mentioned. A broad interpretation of this is an absence of trouble and problems, suggesting a viable household. Luck could be attributed to having great flatmates or could equally mean that those feeling blessed are good housemates themselves. Low expectations and the knowledge that things can easily go "badly wrong", perhaps due to a proliferation of horror stories about "flatmates from hell", prompt contented sharers to consider themselves fortunate. Ben stating that all of his flatmates have been friends implies that such serendipity may not be as guaranteed living with strangers. By residing in a small town you are not likely to move in with anyone, you don't know as chances are that you would know, or know of, other people of a similar age.

Lisa, new to the same town, with limited networking resources, detailed a distressing experience of moving in with strangers. She concluded that given the intense psychological stress the circumstances induced she would never again flat with strangers.

I will never ever ever
move in with a bunch of strangers
never I will not do it
I would rather grow poor thanks
so there is my six month tale of how
what started as a bed of roses
has ended up in thorns basically
you can imagine what I was like
by the end of it and why I wanted out
I just couldn't handle it, my sanity was slipping

Key points here are the emphatic nature of intention to avoid living with strangers in the future; the many months of the unfolding "tale"; a preference for poverty rather than going through such an experience again and compromised mental health. The intensity of the statements remove any suggestion of future compromise. With threats to mental health the only reasonable solution is to move out. Clearly, moving in with unknown people involves risk, yet some participants professed an inclination for flatting with strangers and some, like Julie, justified their preference.

I actually prefer flatting with strangers
you get to make new friends with them
but if you live with friends
sometimes it can ruin a friendship

Making new friends through flatting was frequently stated and often leads to the broadening of social networks through meeting friends of flatmates. Ruining friendships by sharing households was commonly cited as a reason for avoiding flatting with friends, while others felt friendships deepened. Julie precedes her statement with "sometimes", thereby emphasising the possibility of friendships being compromised. There are arguments for both sides: having considered Julie's case for randoms we now also consider the alternative. Postgraduate Sean provides some balanced commentary on both the pros and cons of sharing with friends.

Rule number one was don't flat with friends
because apparently it destroys social relationships
we didn't find that so much . . .
I know some people like to flat with strangers
because they feel that because they're disconnected
they don't have some sort of social relationship with them
they don't have any reservations about telling them to do their dishes

or I want to be left alone after 10 o'clock
whereas friends it can be a bit harder to negotiate
and communicate that through to them

Kirsten Natalier notes that there are no definitive blueprints of rules for sharing.[14] Nevertheless, young adults cope by experimenting and setting their own rules, very often unstated and consistent with individual flat requirements. Broad guidelines, which hopefully smooth the way for the flat to flourish, were spoken of by other participants and give credence to Norman Fairclough's assertion that in everyday practice people actively create a world bound by rules.[15] Significantly, Sean is a city dweller. We found a clear divide between town and city preferences: town folk predominantly favour flatting with friends or at least people they know, whereas city dwellers are more open to living with strangers. Although Sean questions the rule about never flatting with friends, his acknowledgement of this supports the general trend that city flatters are more likely to flat with strangers.

With the proviso of respect for privacy, most people enjoy social connection with flatmates. Sean explains that some individuals deliberately remain detached. In this way relationships can be maintained on a level uncomplicated by friendship. Established social relationships can compromise the need to manage simple housekeeping and the business of sharing with others: communicating and negotiating potential domains of conflict can be difficult. Phoebe contributes more insight into the benefits of living with strangers.

Just because you are friends with someone
doesn't necessarily mean you're going to flat well
with them and I've found that the best flatmates I've had
are people who I didn't know before
and so you don't have any expectations to live with . . .
friendship may or may not build from there
so I think it is better to do it that way round
whereas if you've known someone
for a while I think you kind of expect
them to behave in a certain way
and sometimes it can be very different in reality

There are valid points here as to why strangers make better flatmates. Firstly, friends do not necessarily make good flatmates. Secondly, you have no preconceived expectations of strangers compared to the expectations of people already known. Thirdly, as Sean states, you can communicate your expectations before friendship gets in the way. Fourthly, there is a possibility of friendship growing from daily contact. Lastly, the reality of living with friends may not match assumptions and raises the possibility that good mates can turn into domestic slobs. This relates to the common understanding that you don't get to know someone fully until you have lived with them. Living with someone provides a more complete picture of who they are.

Peter Kemp and Julie Rugg found that people in the UK prefer to flat with friends, arguing that living with strangers can involve insecurity, risk and loneliness.[16] Whereas this was evident in our study, a more complex picture has emerged with no clear trend, with some firmly avoiding combining domestic arrangements with friendships. The contradictory positions of preference for living with friends and the desire to avoid compromising friendships underpin the critical importance of friendship in the lives of young adults. Where there is a friendship there is already trust and communication, both important in functional flats, but good friends do not always translate to good housemates. Emotional intimacy (friendship) provides no guarantee of successful domestic intimacy (sharing). A friend who turns out to be a lazy flatmate can be seen as a betrayal of friendship.[17] Some friendships may not survive the strain of shared domesticity but other friendships may be deepened.

In New Zealand preferring friends as flatmates was the norm among town flatters, where everyone tends to be acquainted. City folks were more open to flatting with strangers, possibly because flexibility and mobility are important for young people, who need to be responsive to the employment market.[18] Young folk often move to larger cities for work or study but they don't have the friendship base that perhaps is available for young adults who remain in smaller urban centres. House sharing is one way of making friends and broadening social circles when moving to a new city.

Kemp and Rugg have noted that expectations of flatmates are more important than preferences.[19] Common expectations as to the degree of cleanliness, tidiness or closeness expected are a dominant explanation for desirable housemates and functional flats. Arguably expectations are easier to communicate to strangers. However, there are uncertainties involved in sharing with strangers, which can impact negatively on psychological well-being. The contradictory aspects of these two different preferences speak to the convolutions involved in sharing, where even generalised rules like not mixing friendship with domesticity are contested. What does not (often) work and what can compromise household and friendship dynamics may ultimately rest on the specifics of which friends and which flats. Dynamics vary from flat to flat and change when a new person moves into a household. Graduate student Pia spoke of a mutual friend joining their happy household only to find that she was increasingly excluded from the activities of the other two, a lonely and bewildering experience.

Interpersonal relationships in the intimacy of domesticity are at best complicated and at worst highly conflictual. As such, young adults seek to avoid unnecessary complications. One aspect which requires careful consideration is the option of flatting with couples or singles.

Singles versus couples

Advertisements for potential flatmates frequently state, "No couples". In our research, singles commonly expressed an aversion to flatting with couples. The following excerpts give insight into why singles prefer to share with other singles. Several potential problems for singles sharing with couples are raised.

Phoebe, having previously flatted as part of a couple herself, explains her preference for single housemates.

I think that you do end up
living in your bedroom a lot more
when you're a couple potentially
because I think that you have that person to
converse with and be with
whereas if you're on your own
you're more likely to seek someone else
to hang out with so you're more likely
to go and sit in the living room

Phoebe observes that couples tend to retreat to their bedrooms and are less likely to seek out company or frequent communal areas. With limited couple presence in communal areas, socialising for single flatmates is restricted. One single-person living with a couple is particularly unsatisfactory. Pia speaks of two of her friends, Emma and Kylie sharing a flat with Kylie's boyfriend.

It was apparently horrible
they all hated living two people and one couple
because Emma and Kylie
they're best friends as well
so it was just real weird dynamics I think

Pia attributes the unpleasant situation to strange dynamics with domestic bliss compromised for all. There are a number of possibilities for the mix being unworkable. As Phoebe mentions, couples tend not to socialise quite as much but the situation is complicated by the girls being best friends, meaning that the boyfriend could also feel excluded. Pressure on Kylie to spend time with both the boyfriend and Emma possibly leaves little time for herself. Pia also explains that tensions within couple relationships can be uncomfortable for flatmates, especially when they are good friends.

I find that quite difficult
to take a side between two people
who are really good friends with me

Getting involved in a couple's problems is not ideal, particularly where it is difficult to avoid one or the other when living with both. Ideally, remaining neutral should not threaten a good friendship with either but this position requires backbone and firmness. Pia also mentioned her flatmate being perpetually suspicious that her partner and Pia secretly fancied each other. The risks to flat stability posed by divided loyalties and jealousy further add to the complex dynamics of sharing.

These tensions possibly explain Chloe's criterion that couples need to be in a stable relationship.

I'm living with my boyfriend in the flat
and no one seems to have an issue with it
but I wouldn't mind living with another couple . . .
as long as they're in a stable relationship

Chloe implies acceptance within their household of living with a couple. The proviso that a couple's relationship should be stable appears a reasonable requirement but ongoing romantic euphoria is not assured. Earlier, Chloe mentioned that she did not like overly social flatmates as she and her partner spent much of their time in their bedroom and preferred quiet housemates, who were "happy to do their own thing". This supports Phoebe's assertion that couples socialise less. Sophie McNamara and John Connell suggest that shared housing can relieve some of the pressure of living as a couple but this does not take into account the negative aspects of singles living with a couple.[20]

A significant threat that can arise from living with a couple is the potential for couples to team up against single flatmates. Counsellor Tim shares a household with his girlfriend, Maree, and one other flatmate.

I could convince Maree of something
then we've got two votes and Mark has one
and that's not necessarily a fair way
to think about things and it's also nice
to have someone on your side
I think there is some strength in that
and for a larger flat if there is conflict
you can kind of feel that you
have someone to back you up
if there is an issue that perhaps
you might not have raised otherwise

Tim acknowledges that there can be a power imbalance when a single person flats with a couple because of the possibility of a couple overruling a single individual. By understanding the unfairness of this prospect, Tim demonstrates an awareness of fundamental democratic principles in sharing and the unique dynamic that couples bring to shared living. While there is strength in numbers there is the potential for abuse of power. Tim also notes the advantage couples could have in having the confidence of a united front to discuss issues that might not otherwise be addressed. This is specifically in the context of a larger flat where, in the event of tension, there is no guarantee of support from others.

Single Julie has flatted for well over a decade and is adamant that she will not flat with a couple. She maintains that living with a couple can give rise to "issues" not encountered in a household of singles. Julie also touches on a couple's capacity for misuse of power.

> *I guess it really depends on their personality*
> *like if they're really lazy or something like that*
> *and then they'll be like*
> *we did the dishes last week*
> *or something like that*
> *I think that that would be an issue*
> *like if they sort of back each other up*
> *when they're both as messy or disrespectful*
> *they'll always back each other up*
> *but they won't go into bat for you*

Flaws of laziness, messiness or disrespect are more difficult to counteract if you are in a minority. These particular negative qualities, detrimental to smooth household functioning, were frequently used to describe undesirable flatmates. One interpretation of "we did the dishes last week" is that in taking weekly turns the single person is expected to take on the duty for the full week on her own, while the couple shares the chore. Or having taken on the dishes the previous week renders them exempt from the task for some time. Any interpretation leaves the single housemate at a disadvantage, potentially exploited, and lacking in support in the power imbalance inherent in sharing with a couple.

From these excerpts it becomes clear why "No couples" is frequently seen in advertisements for house sharing. While couples were not averse to flatting with other couples, experienced single flatters avoid sharing with couples for good reason. Particularly unattractive is one single flatmate sharing with a couple. In addition, two single flatmates starting a romantic relationship was reported as upsetting established equilibrium in interpersonal domestic relationships given the problems that can arise from sharing with couples. A predominant reason for choosing to flat is the attraction of a ready-made social life at home, alleviating loneliness. Living with couples reduces opportunities for socialising.

A further disadvantage is the risk of being involved in a couple's relationship problems. Whereas single people can retreat to their bedrooms, couples invariably share a room, which may intensify any problems they have. Remaining neutral in the affairs of a couple may be wise for flatmates but can be stressful.

One negative aspect raised by both couples and singles was the potential for a couple to exert disproportionate power in the flat. Couples have superior numbers in any decision making, rendering a single person vulnerable to possible disadvantage in decision making and power dynamics within the shared house. For couples there can be strength in numbers in times of conflict but for singles the unequal power balance can be intimidating and unfair. Nevertheless, couples did recognise that combining their vote to defeat single flatmates is not conducive to good flat relationships. Much depends on the characteristics of the couple themselves. The fair-minded realise that superior numbers raise the possibility of inequality in a supposedly egalitarian situation, where all are expected to contribute and benefit equally.

Undoubtedly misleading in discussions of desirable flatmates is the assumption that there is always the option of choice in deciding who to flat with. Practical advice on flatting, and reason, suggests that the answer is to choose flatmates wisely but careful selection of flatmates is not always possible.[21] Economic expediency frequently results in taking in or moving in with any person(s) available at short notice. In addition, errors of judgement in selecting flatmates are always possible, and not evident until well into the business of sharing. By this time, while not "too late" it can be difficult to terminate leasing arrangements and informal agreements.

Conclusion

Four key discourses are evident in discussions about desirable flatmates. Firstly, preferred flatmates are similar to each other in a variety of ways. Secondly, it is important to have the same expectations of each other by way of entertaining friends, standards of cleanliness, noise levels, etc. The third discourse is the imperative for mutual trust and the necessity to feel comfortable with flatmates, especially regarding money, personal safety and security. Lastly, ideal flatmates need to be aware of the delicate balance between being sufficiently sociable but independent with acute sensitivity to flatmates' needs for privacy and quiet time. Tensions between these opposing requirements need to be navigated with care, delicacy and respect, and this includes engaging and disengaging from social interaction at times appropriate to flatmates' emotional states.

Fear of flatting with strangers and security risks associated with the unknown are aspects those who prefer flatting with friends cite for their choice. In addition, having an established comfortable intimacy precludes awkwardness. Those pro-strangers cite the difficulty navigating ground rules and dealing with breaches of expectations whereby friendship could be compromised. Existing friendships can either disintegrate or deepen with sharing: friendship can develop and accelerate from living with strangers. In New Zealand, town flatters prefer sharing with friends while city folk are more likely to flat with strangers.

Experienced single people tend to elect to share with unattached peers while couples are not averse to sharing with other couples. Disadvantages of sharing with a couple include the possibility of getting embroiled in couples' relationship problems and couples' potential to subvert the egalitarian nature of flatting through superior numbers.

Pre-existing social relationships and their potential impact on shared living arrangements in deciding who makes ideal flatmates go beyond personal characteristics and similarities. The art of successful flatting is multi-faceted, with some common but also differing ideas as to what works. Clearly, one size does not fit all. There are no certainties. What appeals to some is anathema to others. Participants were aware of the issues associated with the various options: choices are driven by the unquestioned value associated with having a working living arrangement, well beyond the simple but sometimes thorny issues of sharing costs and chores. The latter are considered in the next two chapters.

Notes

1 This chapter is based on two of our journal articles: Vicky Clark, Keith Tuffin, Karin Frewin and Natilene Bowker, "Housemate Desirability and Understanding the Social Dynamics of Shared Living," *Qualitative Psychology* 5, no. 1 (2018): 26–40. Copyright © 2018, American Psychological Association; Vicky Clark, Keith Tuffin, Karen Frewin and Natilene Bowker, "Shared Housing Among Young Adults: Avoiding Complications in Domestic Relationships," *Journal of Youth Studies* 20, no. 9 (2017): 1191–1207. Copyright © Australian Psychological Society, reprinted by permission of Taylor & Francis Ltd, www.tandf online.com/on behalf of Australian Psychological Society.
2 Sue Heath and Elizabeth Cleaver, *Young, Free and Single? Twenty-Somethings and Household Change* (Hampshire: Palgrave Macmillan, 2003).
3 Sue Heath, "Peer-Shared Households, Quasi-Communes and Neo-Tribes," *Current Sociology* 52 (2004): 161–179.
4 Shelley Mallett, "Understanding Home: A Critical Review of the Literature," *The Sociological Review* 52, no. 1 (2004): 62–89.
5 Heath and Cleaver, *Young, Free and Single?*
6 Ashley Humphreya, Ana-Maria Bliucb and Pascal Molenberghs, "The Social Contract Revisited: A Re-examination of the Influence Individualistic and Collectivistic Value Systems Have on the Psychological Wellbeing of Young People," *Journal of Youth Studies* 23, no. 2 (2020): 160–169.
7 Anuradha Choudry and B. K. Vinayachandra, "Understanding Happiness: The Concept of Sukha as 'Excellent Space'," *Reflections: Psychological Studies* 60 (2015): 356–376.
8 Frances Baum, "Shared Housing: Making Alternative Lifestyles Work," *Australian Journal of Social Issues* 24 (1986): 197–212; Heath, "Peer Shared Households."
9 Irwin Altman, *Environment and Social Behaviour* (Monterey, CA: Brooks/Cole Publishing Company, 1975).
10 Anita Fetzer, "'I Think This Is What I Mean Perhaps This Is Too Tough a View of the World But I Often Think . . .' Redundancy as a Contextualization Device," *Language Sciences* 33 (2011): 255–267.
11 Sue Heath, Katherine Davies, Gemma Edwards and Rachel M. Scicluna, *Shared Housing, Shared Lives: Everyday Experiences Across the Lifecourse* (London: Routledge, 2019).
12 Luzia C. Heu, Martijn van Zomeren and Nina Hansen, "Lonely Alone or Lonely Together? A Cultural-Psychological Examination of Individualism – Collectivism and Loneliness in Five European Countries," *Personality and Social Psychology Bulletin* 45, no. 4 (2019): 780–793.
13 Peter A. Kemp and Julie Rugg, *The Single Room Rent: Its Impact on Young People* (York: Joseph Rowntree Foundation, 1998).
14 Kristen Natalier, "'I'm Not His Wife': Doing Gender in Share Households," Unpublished Doctoral Thesis. University of Queensland, 2003.
15 Norman Fairclough, *Language and Power* (New York: Routledge, 2015).
16 Kemp and Rugg, *The Single Room Rent.*
17 Heath and Cleaver, *Young, Free and Single?*
18 David Clapham, Peter Kelso Mackie, Scott Orford, Ian Thomas and Kelly Buckley, "The Housing Pathways of Young People in the UK," *Environment and Planning A: Economy and Space* 46 (2014): 1016–1031.
19 Kemp and Rugg, *The Single Room Rent.*
20 Sophie McNamara and John Connell, "Homeward Bound: Searching for Home in Inner Sydney's Share Houses," *Australian Geographer* 38 (2007): 71–91.
21 Lauren Earl, *Flatter's Survival Guide* (Wellington: Awa Press, 2013).

5

BENEFITS AND CHALLENGES OF SHARING

By focusing on the economic reasons for flatting it is easy to lose sight of the substantial social psychological advantages of sharing. In the previous two chapters, we examined who might contribute to successful co-residence. In this chapter we consider the positive interpersonal aspects of house sharing and whether these social resources are undermined by expectations of equal sharing of essential household tasks. Housework has been identified as the main source of conflict in sharing.[1] In addition, we examine the effectiveness of rosters. Rosters have been mooted as the safest way of overcoming problems with domestic chores, but our research suggests that rosters are ineffective and regarded as counterproductive to freedom and autonomy.

Social psychological benefits of sharing

Relationships in the intimacy of shared domesticity can not only present challenges but also have the capacity for psychological enhancement. Flatting can be an extremely positive experience, providing companionship, friendship and mutual support with flatmates providing a ready-made, easily accessible social life.[2] Sue Heath and Elizabeth Kenyon argue that communal living is not only an adaptation to changes in society but a psychological imperative, a protective buffer against isolation and loneliness and a means of fostering social networks.[3]

Along with financial pragmatism, shared housing is also an appealing social lifestyle. Timothy May, citing Frances Goldscheider, suggests that sharing can be more valued for social benefits than economic expediency.[4] While such advantages have been suggested, Laryssa Mykyta notes that the social benefits and costs of this way of life are not well documented.[5] We sought to build on the existing literature and broaden our understanding of the complex equation of pros and cons of living in close confines with non-family members.

DOI: 10.4324/9781003161370-5

Companionship

Shared housing can be socially rewarding and an antidote to loneliness as suggested by Phoebe:

> *Even if I was in the position to have my own place*
> *I think I'd still want to flat*
> *because of the social aspect of it*
> *being able to come home*
> *have a chat with someone about your crappy day*
> *yeah that social aspect I think I'd miss*
> *because I have lived on my own*
> *in the UK for a little while*
> *and it's quite lonely if you're on your own*
> *in your own place even if you have*
> *an active social life it can still be nice*
> *to have that someone to hang out with*

That sharing is economically essential for Phoebe is acknowledged but then placed in perspective against the social benefits, which speaks to the importance of these. Solo living is clearly unfavourable when contrasted with the social advantages of communal living. While living alone Phoebe "missed" the companionship and the availability of someone to chat to about a bad day at work. The informality of "hang out with" suggests the spontaneity of such interactions within a flat.

By definition, companionship implies alleviation of loneliness and isolation. Counsellor Sam attributes the need for company as a fundamental human condition.

> *As humans we like to have company*
> *so it is nice to be able to sit down*
> *and share a space with people who*
> *you can actually talk to*

People "you can actually talk to" may refer to having articulate, rather than monosyllabic flatmates or it could be the assumption, given that this century has seen increasingly electronic socialising, that face-to-face interaction is valued. A further interpretive possibility is that "talk to", as strongly implied by Phoebe, means someone who is willing to listen. All interpretations speak to the advantages of having others who are willing to participate conversationally and sometimes flatmates can, importantly, provide this benefit.

Companionship is more than a buffer against loneliness and is important for all kinds of reasons; it has positive psychological effects providing pleasurable social interaction, humour and fun, adding to contentment, regardless of stress levels.[6] Comprehensive research indicates social isolation as a predictor of negative psychological outcomes and this equates to the very lack of social interactions in living alone that participants talked about.[7] Not only do shared households combat loneliness but the intimacy of domesticity can lead to the formation and maintenance of significant friendships and extended social networks.

Friendship

Making friends and networking through flatting were prevalent in the data. Members of an all-male student household, who were very positive about their household, list some of the social advantages of sharing.

Jason: *We're all probably*
I'd say like closest mates
since being in the flat together
Owen: *And you get to meet everyone else's friends*
Aiden: *It's definitely more sociable*
than if you had a room by yourself

Again, the sociability of flatting is compared with the solitary prospect of living alone. Becoming best friends by living together endorses the long-standing social psychological theory that proximity fosters friendship.[8] If a potent predictor of friendship is proximity then the intimacy of household sharing would amplify this trend, particularly since living with someone enables more than a superficial appreciation of a person's strengths and weaknesses. An important point is made about extending social opportunities and networking to a wider circle made available through meeting flatmates' friends.

Julie explains the importance of this when moving to a new city:

And we'd get to know everyone else's friends
some of the best friends I have today
are from flatting with randoms
so it does have its social benefits
especially if you move to a city
where you don't know anyone
which is often what's happened with me

Strangers thrown together in group living and subsequently becoming good friends were often noted. Again, this opens up the possibility of piggybacking off existing social networks, which become available through flatmates. For young people with career aspirations, mobility is an advantage in finding work. The social advantages of shared accommodation are possibly more beneficial in places where there are no established acquaintances. Heath and Cleaver[9] note that when moving cities or countries shared accommodation can offer access to a ready-made social life through flatmates, alleviating loneliness, offering friendship and fostering social networks. The experiences of Kiwi flatmates are consistent with this. Participants were unanimous in endorsing the potential social benefits of shared living.

In the next extract, 28-year-old counsellor Sam talks about the road from flatmate to friendship.

> *But it is like you're flat family type of thing*
> *because you can spend a lot of time with your flatmates*
> *you can get to know and understand how*
> *your flatmates are feeling*
> *you hear about their crappy days at wo̊rk*
> *you hear about any troubles that they're having*
> *you hear about the good and bad things*
> *that are going on in their lives*
> *a good flatmate can end up being a really good friend*

Flatmates being considered "family" was frequently alluded to. Situationally, you are likely to spend some time with flatmates and consequently share everyday events, much like family interactions. A good deal of time spent together can involve knowledge and understanding of intimate aspects of each other's lives where feelings and emotions are shared. The interpersonal interactions involved in disclosures, whereby a "good" flatmate is willing to share personal stories, can extend sharing a roof to friendship.

Friendship and bonding are enhanced, maintained and strengthened by rituals and group outings and add credence to our understanding that the significance of flatting goes beyond merely sharing accommodation. Twenty-one-year-old student Toni lives in a predominantly student flat:

> *So we've kind of arranged*
> *on Mondays* (to) *get together*
> *and play games for a couple of hours*
> *and that's quite good because we can come together*
> *and then we can talk about what needs to be done*
> *and then for the rest of the week if we need*
> *we can just do our own thing*

Specific weeknights were often stipulated in explaining the ritual. For example, one flat had pancake Sundays while another made a ritual of watching weekly episodes of *Game of Thrones* together. Such practices are an important emotional glue that binds groups together. It is clear that the Monday night ritual of game playing is a social get-together and also facilitates discussion about what needs to be done in the household in a congenial way. The final line indicates that the need for independence is respected. "If we need" suggests that socialising is not necessarily restricted to Monday nights.

While some sort of socialising is necessary between housemates the degree of fraternising both within and outside the house varies from flat to flat. An all-women's flat regards itself as high on the continuum of socialising, suggesting that sharing a common roof opens up all kinds of positive possibilities. Twenty-two-year-old Tamsin works in newspaper production:

> *We go away on weekend trips together*
> *it's not just living together we actually*
> *live our lives together as well*

Going on weekend trips together typifies the best outcomes that can arise in terms of developing positive social relationships and, ultimately, friendships. Particularly close relationships are implied with an interesting level of social intensity compared with simply sharing common areas of the residence. This degree of psychological intimacy potentially elevates the status of flatmates to something more meaningful and less transactional. Such companionship, friendship and bonds are a natural precursor to another common discourse, the psychological support afforded by flatmates.

Mutual support

Companionship and mutual support are important components of friendship. In a complementary way, companionship and support are equally but differently psychologically advantageous with different effects on well-being. Companionship is aligned with experiencing pleasure and increases the quality of life. Support is protective and contributes to psychological health by reducing the adverse effects of stress by fostering resilience and coping methods. Support facilitates adaptation, reducing threats to well-being and restoring equilibrium.[10] The psychologically positive perception of mutual support as a protective mechanism against stress was evident in many participants' talk.

The ability to come home and "vent" or "rant" about a difficult day was commonly expressed. Project manager Maree, the partner of counsellor Sam, expands on his ideas of the benefit of a domestic audience.

> *You can come home and talk to each other*
> *in the evening it's not just sharing a house*
> (but) *actually having that communication because*
> *sometimes you just want to come home and*
> *vent about your day at work to somebody in person*

Maree draws on a frequent discourse that flatting is not merely co-existence but can afford significant connectedness. Venting is one way of coping with everyday stressors. Shared physical presence facilitates the opportunity to talk over the problems or pleasures of daily life and mobilise social support. "Communication" is a two-way street where listening is as important as talk and assumes that someone will be willing to listen, empathise and understand. At the same time, it allows a speaker to process thoughts and feelings and dissipate tension.

Chloe reflects that solo living lacks the social advantages of communal living:

If someone has a problem
or you just want to hang out with someone
you just go knock on the door
sit down and have a chat
if you were living by yourself
it would get a bit lonely

Chloe's observations incorporate a number of common benefits cited in earlier excerpts: having flatmates to hang out with; someone to chat to and the prospect of loneliness when living alone. The term "chat" captures the two-sidedness of communication. "Knock on the door" not only underscores the sanctity of private space but also implies that, at least with some flatmates, it is acceptable to seek entry into a bedroom for company or to share a worry. The extract speaks to the positives of sharing, not just the space but the more intimate psychological aspects of living with others and enriching the texture of everyday life by offering mutual support.

A mixed-gender household of five students endorsed this while acknowledging social boundaries.

Mathew: *I guess there is always someone around to watch TV*
and quite close that you can talk to
but also that recognition that you're
quite entitled to sit in your room for two days
and just really be by yourself
Emma: *We wouldn't let you do that*
we would check up on you

Common threads permeate Mathew's talk, such as having someone talk to. This could be interpreted as having someone on hand or someone emotionally close to talk to. Emma interrupts his sentence to assert that the housemates would check up on Mathew if he spent too long a period in his room, indicating her concern for the well-being of flatmates.

Emma also expressed the security she felt afforded by her flatmates.

It feels like you're a family
It's like a foundation in your life

"Family" implies a close bond which may include protection and care. "Foundation" is a persuasively potent structural metaphor and signifies a solid core on which everything else is built. From this we infer that Emma is articulating the firm basis gained from her flatmates to withstand the ups and downs of life, suggesting feelings of fundamental trust, comfort, protection and support. Such relational connections offer optimal conditions for well-being and clearly indicate the psychological importance of good flatmates for emotional security. Participants frequently referred to housemates as "family". Such families are defined by sharing domesticity rather than blood relationships.

The developmental transition from adolescence to adulthood is a highly turbulent psycho-social period with many challenges, including resisting peer pressure to engage in risky behaviour, labour entry, career establishment, partnership formation and finding a place to live outside the family home.[11] Flatmates going through the same adjustments are able to understand and support each other. Student participants noted that sharing with others while studying was beneficial. Social support is a psychological resource: a protective mechanism for adapting to stressful situations, which are predictors of negative psychological outcomes such as anxiety, depression, hopelessness, suicidal thought and physical ills.[12] Emotional, informational and instrumental assistance are the most frequently quoted functions of social support. Emotional support is associated with caring, valuing, understanding and encouragement. Informational support is helping people out with facts or advice that may help solve problems and possible courses of action. Instrumental support refers to material assistance with practical problems.[13] Even the perception of available support can be an antidote to stress.[14]

According to Jody Kellas and colleagues, discussing difficulties not only helps individuals make sense of and gain control of their lives but there are also positive psychological outcomes, including increased feelings of well-being, optimism and higher self-esteem and decreased rates of depression.[15] In addition, being able to share and understand everyday trials and triumphs with others promotes closeness and bonding in relationships.[16] In flatting these can be readily available, in-house resources. Flatmates are also reported to care for housemates who are ill or contact parents when concerned about the mental and physical health of housemates. In addition to the psychological advantages of companionship, friendship and support, participants spoke of increased life skills they acquired through flatting.

Increased social skills and self-reliance

This discourse involves enhancement of social, personal and practical skills promoting self-reliance. Younger participants, such as 20-year-old student Justin, note that living in close quarters with others improves interpersonal skills.

> *Presumably you would be better*
> *at handling social situations*
> *if you are constantly essentially in one*

While this is a tentative proposal that flatting experience better equips a person in social situations, increased communication skills and tolerance were common dimensions of the social skills discourse. According to student Jody:

> *I think you learn to communicate with people*
> *and you also learn to be a bit more tolerant*

I've had friends who have gone from living at home
to moving in with their partner
I think they might not learn tolerance

Tolerance is learned out of necessity but over time this becomes much more conditional and, perhaps, ultimately involves reduced acceptance of certain behaviour. This is evident in veteran or seasoned flatters professing that their levels of tolerance decreased the longer they flatted.

Long-time flatter Phoebe speaks of a growing lack of tolerance.

It's like you do definitely see a change as you get older
the longer people have been flatting and the older they are
the less tolerant they probably are of those little things
I think that's why it is important to make sure
you flat with someone who's of a similar age or life stage
cause then you're more likely to be on the same page

Unlike the tentative statements from younger participants, 34-year-old Phoebe makes a categorical statement leaving no room for dispute. The claim is also legitimised by the older age membership category, implying experience and authority on the topic. "Those little things" are not specified but may be linked to age-related interests and values. Phoebe had previously spoken of a younger flatmate failing to secure the premises before going out and contravening the accepted individual shower routine times. The age criterion was the least permeable in terms of desirability of new flatmates and this may be linked to what people are willing to tolerate. The importance of being "on the same page" was a phrase regularly used by participants. This suggests that for veteran flatters the tension between tolerance and impatience can be resolved by living with those well versed in the skills of co-residence.

Thirty-two-year-old Julie feels that flatting becomes both easier and harder with age.

I think it does get easier the older you get
and the more that you do it
but I think at the same time
you kind of get over living with people

Julie's explanation about why flatting becomes easier is that the longer you flat, the more direct you become about communicating the expectations of flatmates. This supports younger participants' assertions that communication skills improve. Older flatters suggested good communication helped delineate boundaries of "*what is OK and what is not OK*". Older participants did indicate that there comes a time when flatting becomes less attractive possibly through social pressure. Certainly, Sue Heath and colleagues found that older sharers sometimes were very careful about divulging their sharing status because of negative reactions from others.[17]

Running an efficient household requires some skill. That domestic capability is developed in flatting is apparent in student Mathew's pride in graduating from hotdogs to more complex dishes.

if we think back to the first two weeks we were all here
I think we've definitely improved (from)
essentially hotdogs to what I cook now

This household takes turns in cooking for each other. The implication is that the meals of the first few weeks left a lot to be desired. There was much teasing about Mathew's early cooking attempts. Cooking is a useful skill and denotes confidence gained in self-reliance.

This is borne out by postgraduate student, Pia.

I think it kind of grounds you a lot more
in what you're able to do for yourself

Earlier Pia spoke of adjusting to being far away from home with the mutual support of flatmates in her first year of study. After five years of sharing, Pia sees flatting as the foundation of her present self-sufficiency, independence and resourcefulness.

The learning new skills discourse has several dimensions. Firstly, navigating everyday encounters with flatmates and developing compromises, thereby increasing social skills is an important advantage in other spheres of life. Sharing domesticity increases communication and negotiating skills, both highly valued in the workplace, with positive implications for other relationships as well.[18] Effective communication, which contributes considerably to social interactions, was extensively recognised as a necessity among flatmates. Whereas young participants felt their tolerance for others improved, veteran flatters maintained that forbearance needs to be qualified. Experience determines what is acceptable or not from flatmates. As Sue Heath and colleagues note, sharers learn by doing.[19] Participants acknowledged that through flatting they gained practical coping skills, such as cooking. Competency in domestic, social and emotional spheres adds considerably to tools of survival and contributes to a feeling of self-reliance, confidence and control over life.

A further positive that can be noted here is that several participants mentioned that through flatmates they broadened and expanded their cultural horizons by being introduced to housemates' interests, ideas and music. Paul, working in the music media and sharing with an astonishing 21 housemates, when asked about reasons for sharing, prioritised the social side of sharing:

I think economic reasons probably not so much
living the way that we do definitely makes it a lot cheaper
but for most people it's not necessarily about that
it's more about the living environment

and being around so many interesting people
because everyone here is from quite interesting backgrounds
and are quite open about their hobbies
and different outlooks on life
I think definitely people live here for the social aspect of it

Student Toni spoke of being exposed to Live Action Role Play (LAPING) by flatmates, who dress up as fictional characters, re-enacting scenes from novels. She felt this significantly broadened her horizons. Having a flatmate interested in identifying fungi prompted another to take up mycology as a hobby. Having hobbies and interests are important for well-being and enhance the overall quality and enrichment of life.[20] In addition, being introduced to new ideas and interests broadens the mind and facilitates tolerance and compromise.

The above excerpts confirm a number of positive social psychological benefits to shared living: companionship, friendship, mutual support and acquiring social and practical skills, which contribute to self-reliance. Contrastively, not all talk dealt with the positive advantages of flatting since sharing involves responsibilities, such as equal contribution to household chores. The simple necessities of, "Who will take out the rubbish or clean the toilet?" can destabilise relationships, which can swiftly fall apart.

The challenge of communal cooperation with household chores

Contravening contractual obligations corrode the positive attributes offered by flatting. Reciprocity in household work is the norm in shared households, with egalitarian expectations of labour division. Unlike traditional familial households, where cultural expectations have to a large extent dictated who does what, there are often no set rules in shared flats. Tensions as to who does what cannot be avoided by adhering to traditional cultural hierarchies.[21]

Thirty-four-year-old project manager Lucy felt she was at a stage where she could afford an apartment on her own but preferred the space of a shared villa and social aspects of flatting. Nevertheless, she spoke of the challenges of shared household living:

You still have those challenges of
living in a shared housing situation where
not everyone's as considerate as others
so there can be conflict because
someone doesn't pull their weight . . .
I had to keep prompting him to do stuff
tidy, put his stuff away
do the house chores or clean up

Differences are difficult to circumnavigate. While some individuals are considerate others are less thoughtful and this can involve conflict. Inconsiderate people were frequently described as those who fail to "pull their weight", thereby contravening egalitarian norms around household contributions and duties. The challenge lies in trying to get recalcitrant flatmates to cooperate, but this is not always successful. Lucy was not alone in objecting to having to resort to "*parenting*" or "*mothering*" housemates.

In particular, the single most dominant contributor to dissatisfaction with housemates is neglecting dishes. Counsellor Sam talks of the frustration of a flatmate, in the past, who acknowledged being in the wrong but did nothing to rectify the situation.

She would agree that that was her mess
that she was meant to clean it
but wouldn't and so in the end
we had no plates because we were dumb
these are the rules
you have to clean up after yourself
and none of us were willing to
become her housecleaners
and clean up after her so I took
all of the dirty dishes that she had left
for the month on the kitchen bench
and put them on her bed
she didn't make her bed

"In the end we had no plates" suggests that the flatmate's dirty dishes were left for her to do until the supply of clean plates had been exhausted. Sam puts this down to collective foolishness for allowing the non-compliant flatmate to get away with the violation of the rules. Understandably, no one is willing to continually clean up after an errant flatmate. The detail of dirty dishes "left for the month" and not making her bed adds substance to the characterisation of the flatmate as problematic. Although the account is humorous the exasperation is apparent.

According to midwife Annie, vexation in the intimacy of domesticity is difficult to ignore and can impact interpersonal relationships and exacerbate tensions.

If someone doesn't do something
you start getting annoyed with them
because they are in your face all the time

Whereas proximity can foster closeness[22] the opposite is equally true: propinquity increases the chances of people becoming enemies.[23] Significantly, it is the failure "to do something" that causes displeasure, highlighting the frustration of living with those who do not cooperate but reap the benefit of others' labour.

An all-male student flat discusses the negative aspects of living with someone who does not take equal responsibility for housework.

Jason: *We had a flatmate last year*
he isn't with us this year
he was quite lazy
it was quite stressful (for) us
coming to grips with thinking about
how we were going to tell him that
we didn't want to flat with him next year
Noah: *Yeah it's quite stressful*
when someone doesn't pull their weight
and you're pissed off with him
Jason: *And we don't want to make it*
uncomfortable for one another

Past unpleasant experiences are frequently employed as a means of illustrating a point, particularly in group interviews, where airing grievances against current flatmates are understandably avoided. The anxiety associated with raising concerns is evident: dealing with problematic flatmates is stressful. There is recognition that voicing dissatisfaction can make other flatmates uncomfortable, especially since feeling at ease in a flat is deemed a necessity for amicable sharing. The term "pissed off" conveys considerable anger at someone failing to do their share of housework. In addition, the anticipation of having to tell somebody they have been rejected is never an easy conversation to have.

It has been mooted that the more sociability and communication among flatmates, the easier it is to deal with the division of labour and potential discord, but there are those who consistently fail to conform to expectations of reciprocity.[24] Diligent flatmates enhance flat functioning but good natures can be exploited by the unscrupulous, who do not adhere to the communal ethic.

The positive social aspects of shared living can be subverted by domestic conflicts, often involving the day-to-day demands of housework. If all participate equally, then all benefit.[25] Those who consistently fail to contribute are a source of tension. Stress arises not only from conscientious housemates having to do extra work but also from the prospect of confronting the offender or the prospect of asking a flatmate to move out or regrouping without the uncooperative individual. Tolerance may be a valuable asset gained from flatting but does not extend to routinely cleaning up after others. Dismantling an established household to regroup or asking someone to move out has added complications. For young people already economically compromised moving entails financial costs, adding to the stress. Asking someone to move out means finding a replacement with no guarantee that the new flatmate will be a good fit for the flat dynamic. In a talk about household chores, considerable attention was centred on the merits or disadvantages of rosters as a means of assigning housework.

Rosters[26]

The roster or chore wheel (Figure 5.1) indicates who is responsible for a certain task, such as taking out the trash or vacuuming for the week1.

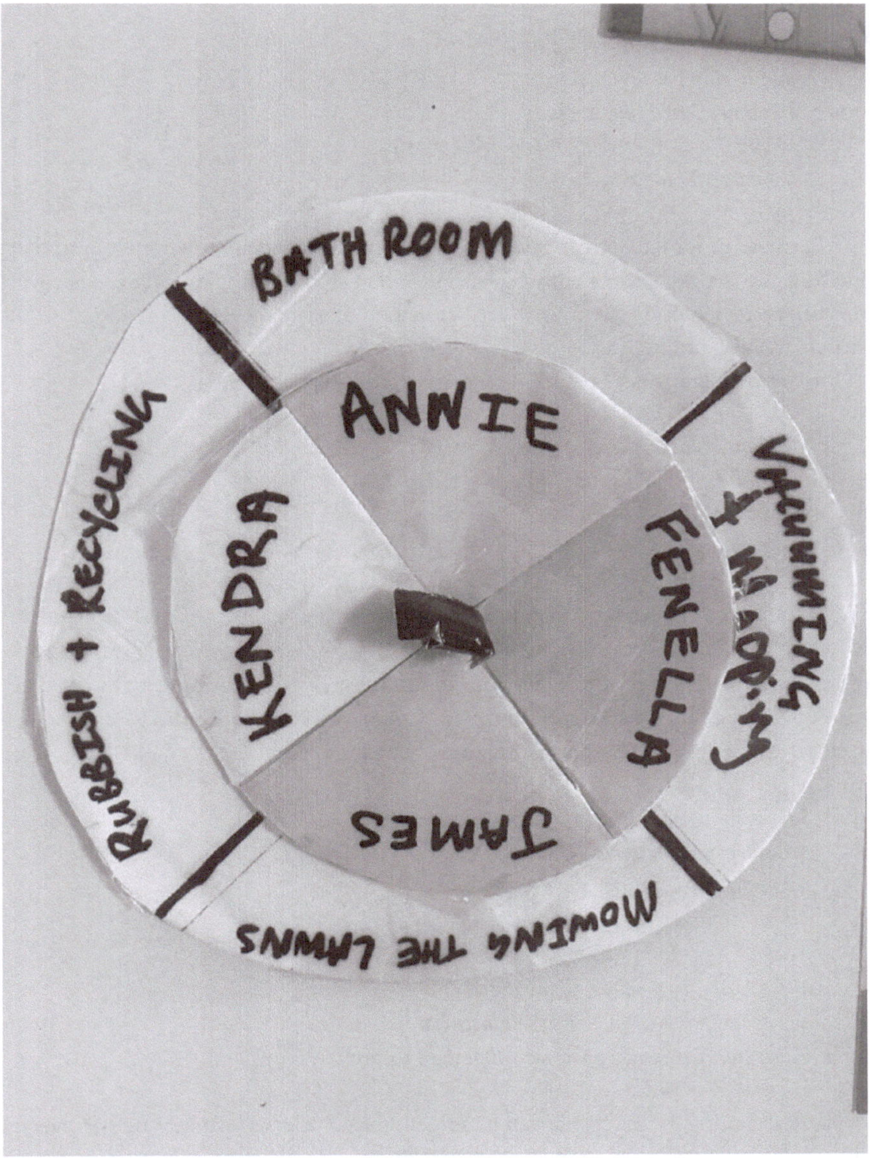

FIGURE 5.1 An example of a chore wheel roster not connected to any of the participants or flats interviewed.

Rosters do not work

The predominant consensus is that chore rosters, as illustrated in Figure 5.1, do not work. In asserting that rosters are ineffective, alternatives for what does work are invariably suggested. One argument is that people are more likely to cooperate if they can utilise their strengths and preferences.

Mike: *We tried a roster just for a little bit*
and it didn't really work
Susie: *No cause Mike likes cooking*
so you'd mainly cook and then other people
would prefer to clean up

Almost without exception participants had tried rosters before concluding that they did not work. Policeman Mike implies that it did not take long to discover the futility of rosters. Communal goals can be better achieved by making use of particular skills and inclinations.

Project manager Lucy speaks of "a great flatting experience".

We didn't have a cleaning roster
we all did stuff and slipped into
the areas that we liked doing
and it all worked

Cleaning rosters are not necessary when flatmates cooperate and are free to do what they enjoy, creating a workable situation without any formal regulation. When strict rosters are introduced very often the precise intention is to encourage shirking flatmates to share responsibilities. A very visible roster in Lucy's flat was an attempt to get a past unhelpful flatmate to contribute to housework.

I set it up when we had the previous flatmate
the other male flatmate
because I do not want to be the person
running round cleaning this place
we're all equally in this together
and so I set it up so it's all organised
and there's no questions who's doing what
it was an interesting experiment that didn't work

Ideally, flatting is an egalitarian arrangement. Understandably, Lucy is averse to being solely responsible for housework. Lucy added that prior experience had taught her that some individuals attempt to avoid housework without attracting attention to their shortcomings. Rationally, a roster should leave no room for uncertainty about duties but some flatmates remain seemingly oblivious to exploiting the time, energy and goodwill of others. Those who ignore chores are as just as likely to ignore rosters.

A recurring reason for flatting is escaping the demands and often narrow confines of the parental home. The anticipation of a life free of structures, rules and obligations makes flatting appealing. Consequently moving into an establishment where there are too many restrictions and claims on time is unattractive.

In rejecting rosters midwife Annie speaks for her flatmates in asserting not only the freedom of moving out of the family home but also a sense of having more control and self-determination over their own lives.

I think freedom is very important
we've moved out of home
we don't live with our parents
it's good to feel like you've got some control
we've already got our jobs and shit
you don't need other stuff
we want to come home
and actually be able to relax
and not have all these duties

The implication is that living with parents is rule-bound with restricted autonomy, whereas flatting offers liberty. "All these duties" suggest that there could be a multitude of tasks to be tackled with the imposition of rosters, seriously curtailing relaxation. A home is a place for destressing, not a place to be burdened with yet more rules and responsibilities. Annie's flatmate, Tamsin, contrasts the difference between flatting with peers and living with her mother, who expected housework to be executed every Sunday.

If I was hungover
or out doing whatever I wanted
she'd get really angry at me
we don't have that here
it's not like you have to
do the bathrooms this week
if the bathrooms don't get done
well they just don't get done
they not ever completely disgusting
it's just that sometimes
we have to factor in life

In this rather humorous account, maternal prioritising of housework over coping with hangovers and social life is regarded as unreasonable. Rigid expectations are contrasted with a more flexible approach, which allows some latitude. This is supported by the reassurance that unacceptable standards are avoided and forestalls any suggestion that conditions deteriorate to the unhygienic. The vagaries and unpredictability of life are a good reason for relaxed attitudes to chores.

Counsellor Sam suggests that life does not subscribe to routines and schedules.

For me life doesn't fit to a schedule
it might be that on my scheduled night
a Wednesday I would rather be out
doing something else
and I would not want to be at home
cooking dinner for flatmates

Participants often qualified justifications for opinions as personal preferences allowing for the possibility that others might not share their views. This averts suggestions of dogmatism, while still managing to make a point. Sam's view emphasises the need for duties to be managed flexibly rather than by a "schedule", which does not allow personal variations. Being tied to a roster when there are more attractive alternatives curtails freedom.

An ad hoc approach emerged as a common way of coping with the demands of housework, without exerting pressure on housemates. Chloe, who appeared to be the matriarch in her student flat, also stated that rosters do not work.

I tried rosters
but it's better just (to) *say,*
"*We'll do the inside work*"
like two of us and the other two
will do the outside work
and then when it needs doing
whoever didn't do it last does it
that way no one feels pressured
and that sort of works out a bit better
it's a bit more relaxed

Chloe may have experienced some difficulty getting flatmates to cooperate as "I tried rosters" implies attempts to find a solution to a problem. Since rosters failed, a more workable alternative is a spoken agreement. The excerpt also demonstrates that some form of yard work may be required. The word "flat" may conjure up apartment living, which is the original meaning of the word, but the term flatting often includes houses with gardens, which need maintenance. Outdoor work may be unappealing to some but attractive to others, who may prefer this to housework. "Pressured" and "relaxed" reinforce the antipathy to stress-inducing structures and deadlines. "Sort of works a bit better" implies that there are still issues with fulfilling responsibilities and completing mundane chores.

"Mental" or "spoken" rosters and collective action appear to alleviate rigid requirements. This was the view of an all-male student flat who found that the roster they tried when first moving in together lasted less than a week due to other commitments. A mental inventory is kept of who has dealt with a chore with the understanding that someone else will perform the task next. Failing that everyone pitches in to clean the flat and the failure of one person to help out is quite evident.

Noah: *It's just kind of easy*
if we just all do the same thing
Jason: *You can't really duck out*
then if you do it's a big deal
Miles: *It's quite obvious*
that you're not helping

This extract speaks to the level of social accountability in sharing. Life is easier for this flat if chores are done collectively and there is more likelihood of noticing the constant absence of a particular person. According to Aiden, from the same flat, there is another limitation of rosters:

I guess when one person
doesn't do their job of the week
everyone else kind of slacks off

If rosters are not adhered to by one person there is the propensity for others to use this as an excuse to reduce their efforts, which can subvert the domestic process. Inherent in these examples is the subtle surveillance of other flatmates' contributions: a policing of others to ascertain if they are doing their duties. If others do not measure up then there is sufficient cause to abstain or only partially complete duties.

If rosters are used they need to be flexible

A less dominant discourse is that if rosters are employed there is a need for flexibility. This is closely aligned with the notion that life does not operate to schedule; allowances must be made for other demands on time. A mixed student flat did have a roster but it was not strictly policed.

Greg: *We have pretty loose rosters*
Mathew: *Generally we have sort of*
rosters in place there's expectations
like if it's a Tuesday then I'll be cooking
and then we have a chore wheel essentially
but it's always
Justin: *It's flexible*

Essentially, the chore wheel is fluid with everyone included in these expectations but flexibility acknowledges that life does not run to schedule and exceptions need to be made with some swapping of duties to accommodate preferences and the unexpected. Sam, along with other participants, stressed that the effectiveness of rosters is limited without communication.

Once you're living in shared spaces
you have to communicate
otherwise things can go horribly
there's only so much that a roster
on the fridge can actually achieve

The ability to communicate effectively was frequently cited as essential for functional shared households. Without this ability, there is potential for misunderstanding, tension and conflict. This "horribly" invokes unpleasantness, particularly unsettling in homes, which should represent a sanctuary of relaxation and destressing from the everyday ups and downs of life.[27] In addition, rosters do not guarantee that chores will be performed to an acceptable standard. Sue Heath et al. note that equal willingness and agreement as to how and when cleaning is required are rare.[28] Conflict can result from different ideas as to what constitutes cleanliness; discussion can clarify common expectations regarding satisfactory standards.

Paul lives in an astonishingly large household, which does operate a functional roster:

We have a system here where
if you don't do your chore
for the week you get charged $15
and it goes up on the board
and someone else can pick up that chore
and they can get a $15 credit
so that system keeps the house really tidy
I've lived in a lot of houses
and living with 21 people
surprisingly is the probably the cleanest house
I have ever lived in

With a large number of residents the house has a constitution, which determines behaviour. Not only does failure to do chores result in a fine for slackers but also those financially constrained are able to earn some extra money.

In a seminal study on shared housing, in which she identified factors contributing to successful sharing, Frances Baum concluded that while some flats functioned well on an ad hoc system, rosters were the "safest" means of coping with household chores. In addition, Baum found that some people were ill-disposed to the regimentation of rosters. In her study of 11 mixed-gender households, Kirsten Natalier found only one operated successfully with a roster. Rebecca Williamson, similarly, noted that rosters may be regarded by some as democratic but authoritarian to others, compromising personal responsibility, autonomy and independence.[29]

The dominant discourse from our research is that rosters are ineffective and unpopular with young adults seeking freedom and independence. Freedom does not mean an absence of accountability but formal rosters are not necessary with responsibility and cooperation. Young adults seek to prevent domestic chaos by adopting a more flexible approach. This can be achieved by utilising preferences, strengths and pitching in when someone else is clearly working towards tidying or cleaning communal areas. When people took on tasks they enjoyed there was no evidence of precise offsetting of difficulty or time consumption of one chore against another. In addition, it was noted that one advantage of flatting is that when everyone behaves responsibly the tediousness of housework is shared.

Apart from curtailing freedom, rosters are regarded as contributing to stress by not taking other demands into account, for example, being expected to do chores when exams or deadlines loom or visitors arrive unexpectedly. Life does not conform to schedules. Being tied down to duties when more appealing opportunities arise is counterproductive to freedom. In practice, rosters are vulnerable and liable to be subverted by more pressing or likeable activities.

A second, less robust discourse to emerge is that if rosters are employed then flexibility, commitment and sound communication are essential for conveying expectations of acceptable standards of cleanliness and tidiness. Rosters alone cannot achieve this. Success is possible if all members are accommodating, happy with the system adopted and problems are discussed and resolved before tensions become unmanageable. This requires considerable tact and communication skills.

Shared housing presupposes reciprocity of labour and sacrifice of time and energy. A common excuse reported by participants, critical of slackers, is that the culprits considered an assigned task not essential (as in clean enough) or even claimed that someone else had already attended to the chore. In this way responsibility is avoided. Some housemates use the excuse that they do not have the time to do chores while ignoring the fact that their co-residents may also operate within time constraints or that others should not be obliged to make up the deficit. Employing a cleaner can be the answer if no one has the time or an inclination for housework, provided everyone agrees and contributes. However, sufficient funds for this are not always available and more likely when professional people co-reside.

Free riding occurs when an individual is able to profit from a group without contributing a fair share because others will pick up their slack.[30] Those who shirk domestic duties are rewarded with a clean home. For those who do comply there is the risk of the sucker effect. In order to avoid being a sucker, some individuals will reduce or withhold their contribution to the collective good if they believe that another member is free riding.[31] This is evident in our study, where flatmates recognised that failure to do duties by one flatmate could activate non-compliance in others. If every flatmate believes that others are free riding and refuse to do chores, then the resulting dirt and disorder are bound to result in unpleasant and squalid surroundings. Alternatively, the ideal flatmate, who cleans up after others without reciprocation, may not only be altruistic but also be naïve. In the long run, exploitation of the goodwill of others will be paid for when the flat destructs or the opportunist is asked to leave.[32]

If all cooperate equally and fairly in the social contract of shared living then all benefit. Fairness needs to be encouraged to prevent social loafing. Social loafing can be defined as a tendency to reduce effort because the nature of tasks makes it impossible for others to evaluate individual performance.[33] Social facilitation studies indicate that people can be more productive when others are present. Shirkers are more easily identified if all flatmates clean together at the same time, as advocated by participants in this study. This is evident in talk of other flatmates joining in a clean-up when one individual starts the process. In this way authoritarian coercion is anonymous. Surveillance of others' input was clearly evident but there was an aversion to overt policing.

Clearly, living with those failing to do chores presents challenges. It was apparent that systems of dealing with housework were continually being reformed, becoming more restrictive with continued breaches but loosening if people could be trusted to cooperate without coercion. Such patterns of change usually survive only long enough to attend to the current needs of its members. Since flats are frequently transitory establishments, group dynamics are continually changing; when a housemate is replaced it takes time to reform as a workable unit and for a viable household to be achieved.

Conclusion

Given that participants who had experimented with living on their own later returned to flatting because of loneliness, the social advantages of sharing are clearly important. This corroborates the findings that home sharers' experiences are mostly positive and minimally frustrating.[34] Essentially, flats are hospitable environments regarded as home. Nevertheless, the social-psychological positives of sharing are tempered with the potential for upset through someone who disregards expectations of equally contributing to household responsibilities. Whereas rosters have been suggested as a practical way of apportioning tasks, we demonstrate that while theoretically rosters can be useful, practically they are neither feasible nor desirable. If employed, rosters should be flexible. People are more likely to commit to chores they enjoy or prefer doing. A high level of communication, cooperation and responsibility is essential if the day-to-day operation of the household is to function. Households are orderly on their own terms: no particular formula for housekeeping guarantees success but positive payoffs can be achieved by mutually agreed upon strategies. If a common understanding cannot be achieved then the prognosis is poor. With the primary site of interpersonal tension identified as housework, the following chapter examines other areas of potential conflict that can sabotage flat relationships.

Notes

1 Frances Baum, "Shared Housing: Making Alternative Lifestyles Work," *Australian Journal of Social Issues* 24 (1986): 197–212; Sue Heath and Elizabeth Cleaver, *Young, Free and Single? Twenty-Somethings and Household Change* (Hampshire: Palgrave Macmillan, 2003); Kristen Natalier, " 'I'm Not His Wife': Doing Gender in Share Households," Unpublished Doctoral Thesis. University of Queensland, 2003; Karsten Mause, "The Tragedy of the Commune: Learning From the Worst-Case Scenarios," *Journal of Socio-Economics* 37 (2008): 308–327.
2 Mary Elizabeth Hughes, "Home Economics: Metropolitan Labour and Housing Markets and Domestic Arrangements in Young Adulthood," *Social Forces* 81 (2003): 1399–1429.
3 Sue Heath and Elizabeth Kenyon, "Single Young Professionals and Shared Household Living," *Journal of Youth Studies* 4 (2001): 83–100.
4 Timothy D. May, "Shared Housing: The Sharing Economy Gives Roommates a New Image," *Christian Science Monitor*, March 30, 2014, https://news.tfionline.com/post/81379564527/shared-housing-the-sharing-economy-gives.
5 Laryssa Mykyta, "Economic Downturns and Failure to Launch: The Living Arrangements of Young Adults in the US. 1995–2011," *SEHSD Working Paper 2012–2024*. Prepared for the Transition to Adulthood after the Great Recession Conference, Milan (October 25–26, 2012).
6 Karen S. Rook, "Social Support and Companionship: Effects on Life Stress, Loneliness, and Evaluations by Others," *Journal of Personality and Social Psychology* 52 (1987): 1132–1147.
7 John T. Cacioppo and Louise C. Hawkley, "Perceived Social Isolation and Cognition," *Trends in Cognitive Sciences* 13 (2009): 447–454.
8 Leon Festinger, Stanley Schachter and Kurt Back, *Social Pressures in Informal Groups: A Study of Human Factors in Housing* (Palo Alto, CA: Stanford University Press, 1950).
9 Heath and Cleaver, *Young, Free and Single.*
10 Rook, "Social Support and Companionship"; Cacioppo and Hawkley, "Perceived Social Isolation."
11 Jeffrey J. Arnett, *Emerging Adulthood: A Theory of Adulthood From the Late Teens Through the Twenties*, 2nd ed. (Oxford: Oxford University Press, 2015).
12 Marcel Lourel, Anne Hartmann, Caroline Closon, Farida Mouda and Ofelia Petric-Tatu, "Social Support and Health: An Overview for Selected Theoretical Models for Adaptation," in *Social Support and Health: Theory, Research, and Practice with Diverse Populations*, ed Sheying Chen (New York: Nova Publishers, 2013), 1–20.
13 Peggy A. Thoits, "Social Support as Coping Assistance," *Journal of Consulting and Clinical Psychology* 54 (1986): 416–423.
14 Niall Bolger, Adam Zuckerman and Ronald C. Kessler, "Invisible Support and Adjustment to Stress," *Journal of Personality & Social Psychology* 79 (2000): 953–961.
15 Jody Koenig Kellas, Haley Kranstuber Horstman, Erin K. Willer and Kristen Carr, "The Benefits and Risks of Telling and Listening to Stories of Difficulty Over Time: Experimentally Testing the Expressive Writing Paradigm in the Context of Interpersonal Communication between Friends," *Health Communication* 30, no. 8 (2015): 843–858.
16 Duane Buhrmester and Karen Prager, "Patterns and Functions of Self-Disclosure During Childhood and Adolescence," in *Disclosure Processes in Children and Adolescents*, ed Ken J. Rotenberg (New York: Cambridge University Press, 1995), 10–56.
17 Sue Heath, Katherine Davies, Gemma Edwards and Rachel M. Scicluna, *Shared Housing, Shared Lives: Everyday Experiences Across the Lifecourse* (London: Routledge, 2019), 52.
18 Ivana La Valle, Siobhan O'Regan and Charles Jackson, *The Art of Getting Started: Graduate Skills in a Fragmented Labour Market* (London: The Institute for Employment Studies, 2000), Report, 364, www.employment-studies.co.uk/system/files/resources/files/364.pdf.
19 Heath et al., *Shared Housing.*

20 Marjolein C. den Haan, Rens G. A. Brankaert and Yuan Lu, "Applying Design Methods to Promote Older Adults' Walking Activities Based on Their Hobbies and Personal Interests," in *Design of Assistive Technology for Ageing Populations*, eds Andree Woodcock, Louise Moody, Deana McDonagh, Ajita Jain and Lakhmi C. Jain (Cham: Springer Nature, 2020), 257–273.
21 Baum, *Shared Housing*; Natalier, "I'm Not His Wife."
22 Leon Festinger, Stanley Schachter and Kurt Back, *Social Pressures in Informal Groups*.
23 Ebbe B. Ebbesen, Glenn L. Kjos and Vladimir J. Konečni, "Spatial Ecology: Its Effects on the Choice of Friends and Enemies," *Journal of Experimental Social Psychology* 12 (1976): 505–518.
24 Heath and Cleaver, *Young, Free and Single*.
25 Maus, *The Tragedy of the Commune*.
26 The section on Rosters draws on work published by the authors in the Australian Journal of Psychology: Vicky Clark, Keith Tuffin, Natilene Bowker and Karen Frewin, "Rosters: Freedom, Responsibility, and Co-operation in Young Adult Shared Households," *Australian Journal of Psychology* 71, no. 3 (2019): 232–240. Copyright ©Australian Psychological Society, reprinted by permission of Taylor & Francis Ltd, www.tandfonline.com on behalf of Australian Psychological Society.
27 Shelley Mallett, "Understanding Home: A Critical Review of the Literature," *The Sociological Review* 52 (2004): 62–89.
28 Heath et al., *Shared Housing*.
29 Baum, "Shared Housing"; Natalier, "I'm Not His Wife"; Rebecca Williamson, "Flatting Futures: Negotiating Domesticity, Home and Individuality in the New Zealand Flat," Unpublished Master's Thesis. Victoria University, 2006.
30 Elinor Ostrom, James Walker and Roy Gardner, "Covenants With and Without a Sword: Self-Governance Is Possible," *The American Political Science Review* 86, no. 2 (1992): 404–417.
31 Robyn M. Dawes and John M. Orbell, "Social Dilemmas," in *Progress in Applied Social Psychology*, vol. 1, eds Geoffrey M. Stephenson and James H. Davis (New York: Wiley, 1981), 37–65.
32 Mause, *The Tragedy of the Commune*.
33 Bibb Latané, Kipling Williams and Stephen Harkins, "Many Hands Make Light Work: The Causes and Consequences of Social Loafing," *Journal of Personality and Social Psychology* 37, no. 6 (1979): 822–832.
34 Heath et al., "Shared Housing."

6

CONFLICT

The previous chapter examined the potential for conflict over contribution to housework and how this can undermine the social benefits of sharing and the effectiveness of rosters for circumventing problems. This chapter builds on these aspects by including other areas of contention in shared domesticity, where the potential for disagreement and offence can be magnified. Patterns in talk centre on sources of conflict, how differences are managed and the negative repercussions of unresolvable problems.[1] What becomes clear is that young adults seek to avoid or find harmonious solutions to problems. The effect of the physical building lived in on social relationships was broached by participants and this aspect is considered in some detail.

Sources of conflict

Different expectations of cleanliness and tidiness, freeloading and miserliness are common discourses drawn on to explain how conflict can arise among flatmates.

Differing approaches to cleanliness

Similar views as to what constitutes acceptable standards are significant. Having different ideas about what clean means can apply equally to those with questionable standards or the overly zealous. The need for flatmates to be reasonably clean and tidy was common but those who have unrealistic expectations and are too meticulous or controlling are not easy to live with and can create tension. Thirty-four-year-old Lucy recalled being chastised for a minor lapse of standards.

> *I like living in a clean and tidy space*
> *but I wouldn't consider myself to be obsessive*
> *I like places that are lived in*

DOI: 10.4324/9781003161370-6

and she came across more and more like that
I had dinner one night
cleaned my dishes
and left them in the drying rack
to dry while I was watching TV
and I went to bed and left them there
and then I got told pretty quickly that
actually in this house you dry the dishes
and put them away

For Lucy a "lived in" domestic space with adequate sanitation standards is preferable to clinical tidiness. Feeling comfortable with flatmates is a dominant theme in describing desirable flatmates. Comfort is difficult to achieve with standards that are too rigorous, and subsequently, Lucy moved out.

Phoebe also spoke of disputes resulting from different concepts of cleanliness and tidiness.

You just might clash
or have a very different idea of
what clean means
also some people are
much more easy going than others
some people get very angry and frustrated
if you don't put away a teacup
you need to be okay with the occasional
teacup or glass being left out
otherwise you will end up
being really stressed out all the time

That unrealistic expectations can lead to discomfort, disagreement and potential conflict are evident in both the aforementioned examples. Easy going people, who accept minor transgressions, are less likely to become angry and frustrated with positive implications for psychological well-being. Not putting away a teacup illustrates how reactions can differ from trivial violations. Even insignificant matters like this can be amplified in the close intensity of shared living and communal spaces.

Nevertheless, as explained by student Jody, unchecked minor lapses have the potential to escalate.

Personally I don't mind if
people are messy
but I suppose in the communal space
like the kitchen and the lounge
that's where if I leave a mess there
then it's kind of the broken window effect
so one person leaves their glass

and then the next thing you know
the next day there's a plate and a glass
and a knife and a fork and another glass

As opposed to the private space of a bedroom, which can be disorganised, shared areas are governed by different rules. While Jody herself is not obsessively tidy she understands the importance of clean and tidy communal areas. She explains the infectious aspect of how untidiness can encourage further disorder by referring to Wilson and Kelling's Broken Window theory.[2] This theory suggests that norm violation and disarray potentially spread disorder if not checked. Early intervention forestalls further violations and untidiness spreading. Uncontrolled minor matters can be the beginning of something that can escalate into a source of significant and intolerable irritation for some.

A sole person appreciating a clean environment but having little control over the slackness and slovenliness of housemates is distressing, as postgraduate student Pia describes.

There was about six or seven of us
in the same flat and it got absolutely disgusting
and I just hated it because I like things clean
it's their spaces and it was not my place to mother them
to tell them to clean up after themselves

If a neat and orderly flatmate is outnumbered, effectively dealing with the problem is unlikely as the impact of one individual is limited. One of the benefits of flatting is to escape the demands of parents and power structures: stepping into the role of a parent is neither attractive nor desirable. In addition, Pia is aware that it is not her duty to take on a parental role. "Mother" or "parent" are words steeped in cultural ideologies and the terms were used by others to indicate the childlike irresponsibility of some flatmates who need to be prompted to maintain standards. Clearly, flatmates are responsible for cleaning up their mess with the need to respect the rights of others who share communal spaces.

One person talked about her frustration with the disorderliness of fellow housemates and attempt to instil some sense of order. She purchased containers for each flatmate so that when the clutter in shared spaces became unbearable she would put their belongings in their designated containers. Her attempt at order was not well received and was effective only until the containers became too full to add any more objects to them.

Divergent expectations regarding cleanliness can be difficult to resolve. While living with an obsessively clean and tidy housemate can be stressful, the opposite of living with a slothful housemate is also true. Particularly stressful is living with a person with questionable personal hygiene resulting in "*revolting*" body odour. Whereas different understandings of cleanliness and hygiene have been noted in earlier research,[3] our participants highlight the problem of living with flatmates with excessively high standards. Unrealistic demands can be seen as interpersonal rejection.[4] The reason why this is a common complaint could be due to the fact that no one likes to be considered dirty or lazy. By classifying others as hypercritical and meticulous, one's own implied defects can be invalidated. Nevertheless, for those who do like cleanliness and tidiness, dirt and messiness can be a seriously upsetting issue. For those who are not particularly financially flush money issues can also be very distressing.

Economic tensions

There is potential for conflict from those who take financial advantage of flatmates. An unacceptable trait in a housemate is someone who plunders the collective or individual resources of co-residents.

Freeloading

Freeloading is a lack of consideration for equal sharing of communal commodities and costs, such as food, hot water, electricity and broadband. Failure to assume equal fiscal responsibility is in defiance of one of the core principles of successful shared living. In an all-female flat, Donna shares with two others, all are in their early twenties and employed in retail. Two work additional evening shifts in hospitality in order to make ends meet. Despite this the household was sparsely furnished and at the time of the interview they were unable to afford a TV.

We had a pretty crap flatmate that moved in
that we didn't really know
and there was a bit of conflict with him
but he ended up moving out
because he was just very immature
we were paying for the food
because he was doing his own grocery shop
and he would keep eating our food
and using our stuff and so we said,
"Look you either buy the groceries
or you stop eating our food,"
and he said, "Well then I'll just move out"

The negativity associated with this flatmate is his failure to share food costs and thereby expect to have his meals subsidised by the others. The source of this failure is then linked to immaturity and lack of knowledge about him when he moved in. Although the ultimatum was to stop consuming others' food, the freeloading flatmate moved out when challenged.

Flatmates' freeloading love interests are a further source of conflict as explained by counsellor Julie, talking about her student years in a flat.

When you're a student
and money's such an issue and people

are showering at your house
and you are paying for it
and they're not
and he would also eat our food

Impecunious students are particularly susceptible to the depletion of scarce resources. Abuses of others' resources, including showering and food, are mentioned, highlighting additional costs and exploitation involved. Julie did qualify her aversion to freeloading boy/girlfriends in her student years by saying that once embarked on a career path with more disposable income there is some room for latitude with visiting friends. However, according to signwriter Kelly, there are limits to tolerance:

I don't mind the girlfriends coming and staying
or boyfriends in whichever case
so long as it is not every single night
the first boy I had living with me
his girlfriend stayed for three months in a row
she didn't pay rent or anything
so I said to him,
"Look she doesn't need to stay as often
unless she wants to start paying a bit of rent
she's pretty much living here".

The key focus here is the financial cost of having extras staying and not paying. Besides the additional costs carried by Kelly for the live-in girlfriend, she was to all intents and purposes living with a couple. And as we are aware, couples do not make the most desirable flatmates for single people.

Miserliness

While limited budgets necessitate frugality, penny-pinching is not appreciated. Protecting resources from potential plundering by freeloaders may be essential, but tolerance for dealing with minor infringements of food ownership is necessary for maintaining interpersonal relationships. This is reflected in librarian Mary's extract.

I'm not worried if someone
eats my apples or uses my butter
and that sort of thing
I've never been one of those flatmates
who draws a line on the olive oil bottle

Implied in this statement is the notion of some degree of fair give and take and not becoming too precious about minor domestic matters about food ownership. The unnecessary "drawing a line on the olive oil bottle" is humorous but suggests that Mary has come across this sort of behaviour to curb pilfering. Economic prudence may be necessary but miserliness is not an attractive attribute.

This second source of conflict focuses on freeloading and miserliness. Conflict can arise in households that do not share food when individuals consistently consume housemates' food without replacement. In households where food is shared flatmates who consistently eat more than a fair share of food or manage to devour the nicer food before others have a chance to partake are likely to provoke negative reactions. Very often conflict is rooted in issues of fairness. For the economically challenged financial austerity is essential. Conflict resulting from scarce resources is well documented.[5] Visiting partners or friends' use of meagre supplies can create tension, especially among impecunious students. Young professionals may be better able to afford to be more generous but nobody enjoys being exploited. Contrarily, miserliness, such as drawing lines on containers or putting names on food is not acceptable. Subtle differences between frugality and meanness again demonstrate the fine balance required for successful co-residence.

Money

Sharing expenses is vitally important to successful shared living. Student Chloe speaks of those shirking financial or housework responsibilities:

> *I don't know why*
> *but some people when*
> *money comes into it*
> *they don't want to pay a bill*
> *or not on time or not prepared*
> *to put their share into the cleaning or something*
> *they don't want to do their part*
> *it's definitely been the breakdown of it*

Chloe suggests that relationship breakdowns are due to unwillingness to contribute to combined expenses or agreed timing of payments. Besides not paying bills being patently unfair, violation of expectations threatens the cohesion and ultimately the viability of shared living. This also applies to failure to participate in household chores.

There is a need to feel confidence and trust that housemates will meet their financial obligations and remittance deadlines. Failure to do so causes stress and anxiety for those who do comply. Penalties for late payment, such as electricity being cut off, can affect all. Surprisingly, the complaint of non or late payment of rent was rare. Possibly, this is due to young adults being aware of the consequences of non-payment by a housemate and anticipating this possibility by setting up automatic payments. Automatic payments may or may not include electricity. Some flats wait for the monthly power bill while others estimate the monthly electricity bill, pay a set amount and any extra money built up over summer is used to cover the heavier winter bills. If the monthly bill exceeds the set amount then all share the added expense. Such pragmatic arrangements are frequently conditional on joining a household. Financially pre-emptive measures ensure that rent and electricity payments are paid on time, with an assurance of a roof overhead and reliable power.

Policy analyst Lucy speaks of the considerable effort involved in trying to get inconsiderate flatmates to contribute their fair share.

It can be challenging to
try and get that person on board
and alongside the other folks
and sometimes it doesn't work

Getting some housemates to cooperate is problematic and prone to failure. Consideration for others is a prominent discourse regarding desirable flatmates. "Try and get that person on board" in the colloquial sense evokes the necessity for equal participation with other housemates. Not meeting obligations of housework and finances is indefensible: ultimately this is paid for by having to move out or victims decamping to another flat.

Increased tension and conflict resulting in strained interpersonal relationships and compromised trust have the potential to undermine the delicate basis on which shared living operates. How are these threats to household viability managed?

Managing conflict

Two opposing methods of dealing with conflict are evident: while many agree that good communication and talking over problems is the best means of resolution, some prefer to prevent or avoid confrontation.

Occupants of an all-male student flat maintain that they are adept at dealing with conflict by frankly discussing problems:

Miles: Just no secrets
we all just sit down
and talk about it
Noah: We're really good with conflict
like our flat meetings
if we ever need to bring something up
we just do it round dinner
and we haven't had any fights or anything

"No secrets" suggests that a flat policy of transparency and open communication provides a workable system for dealing with issues as they arise. Discussing problems over dinner or other flat gatherings is less adversarial than organising a specific meeting. That no acrimonious exchanges or feuds have developed indicates that a system of open communication is successful.

Twenty-eight-year-old Sam explains that flat meetings can be fruitful but desired results are not always assured.

Communication is good
like hold flat meetings
I've been in flats where things have been
a bit unsteady and if everyone
gathers around the kitchen table and puts
as much as they want to out there
and say, "I don't like that this is happening,"
or "I would like this to change"
that is best case scenario
which has worked in the past
other times they haven't

Like many participants, Sam believes that communication is essential for dealing with tension. If problems are raised and discussed then working through issues is possible, but this requires everyone to participate in the process. While this seems obvious, one participant mentioned the difficulty of having a flatmate who retired to his room whenever anyone tried to broach any difficulties. Nevertheless, while some meetings resolve problems others are not successful. Discussion can be highly uncomfortable and escalate into outright conflict.

Frances Baum found that motivation to share impacts relationships. Those who feel forced to share, through economic necessity, tend to focus on difficulties, regard them as insurmountable and are less willing to compromise. Those committed to the lifestyle regard interpersonal conflict and its resolution as an inevitable challenge.[6]

While talking is regarded as the best method of solving problems, one flat avoided face-to-face confrontation by writing letters to each other when problems arose, each stating their opinion on the issue. This is different to passive-aggressive notes (Figure 6.1), posted around the house to deter offenders.

Dealing with problems this way is particularly disliked. Arguably, such anonymous notes are a way of avoiding confrontation, but in the long run, they can be destructive if fellow flatmates react badly. Another abhorrent practice is to complain about a flatmate on social media rather than address the person directly.

When housemates cannot get past their differences negative conflict occurs, but inevitable tensions in a shared living space can be both positive and productive even when the subject matter is difficult.[7] On the positive side, cooperation in reaching mutually agreed upon solutions with respectful, constructive conversation improves group cohesion and relationships.[8]

One of the positive aspects of flatting identified by participants is that social skills are increased. Negotiating the complex nexus of everyday interactions in the intense arena of domesticity can translate to acquisition of sound interpersonal interactions in both the workplace and relationships in general. Constructive cooperation and collaborative strategies learned through sharing contribute

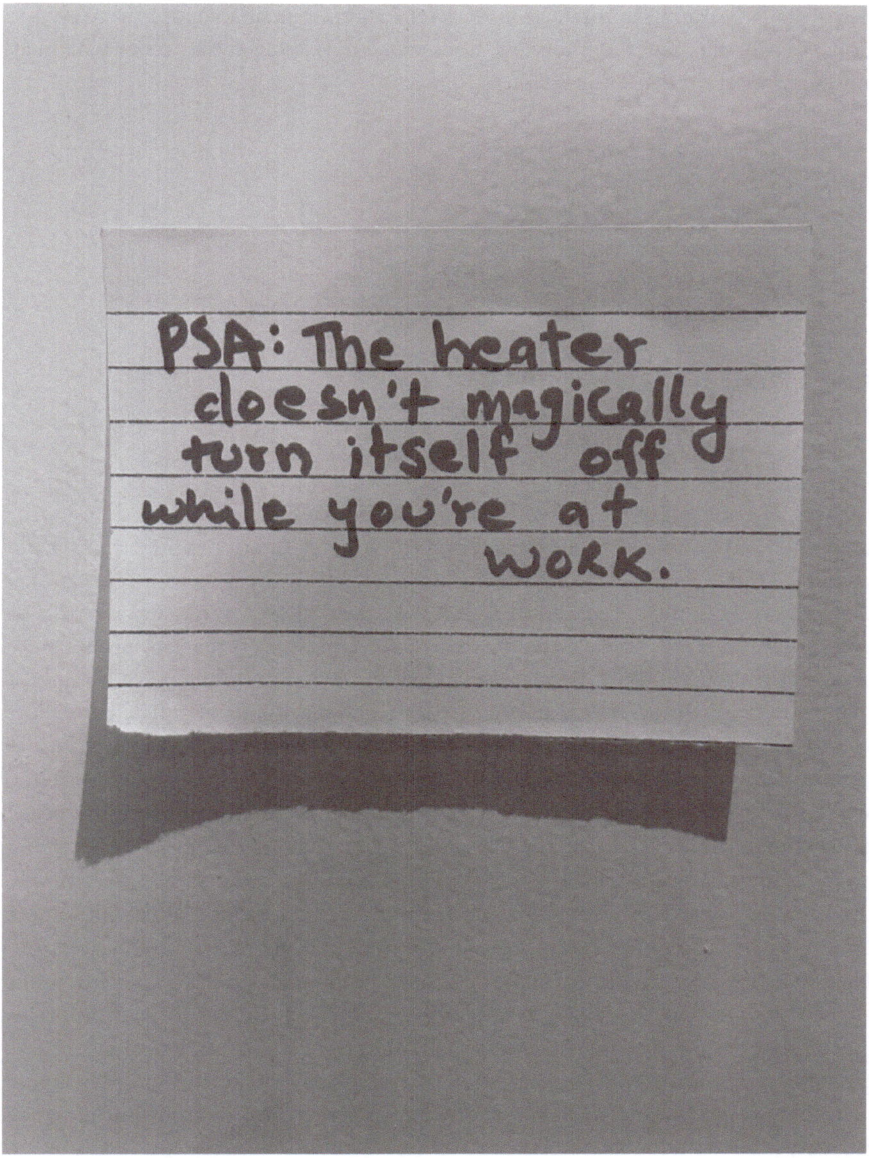

FIGURE 6.1 An example of a passive-aggressive note.

to psychological well-being and can enhance relationships. Conversely, too much negative interaction can undermine morale, reduce teamwork and alienate.[9] Directly addressing issues through communication and group meetings was the dominant solution suggested, but a second competing approach to avoiding problems was also raised.

Avoiding problems has two trajectories. The first is pre-emption of problems by consideration, tolerance and sensitivity to flatmates' moods: knowing when to be particularly careful in interaction or defer contentious or antagonistic conversations. In the following flat interview, housemates agree that awareness of what may annoy or upset others is important.

Annie: *I think we try to avoid conflict*
a lot of the time
I think we're forgiving about
each other's personalities as well
Meg: *Yeah we know what each person does*
and what things get them annoyed
so we make allowances or
Claire: *Yeah you kind of know*
what would annoy Annie or whatever
Tamsin: *You just become a little more considerate*

This all-female flat considered themselves good friends, which may account for the extent of consideration for each other. Annie's statement that they try to avoid conflict is qualified by "a lot of the time", suggesting that there are occasional unavoidable tensions. Being sensitive to housemates' idiosyncrasies and moods was commonly raised in the talk about conflict prevention. Personal pet peeves were also frequently mentioned, suggesting that a small irritation to one person can be a major source of annoyance to another with potential cause for conflict. For example, two housemates enjoy doing jigsaw puzzles as a means of relaxing: one comes from a family where it is considered cheating to consult the picture on the box while this rule never applied in the other's parental home. To preserve the peace the picture examining flatmate only does this when the other is not at home. Being aware of what disgruntles others is important even when the foible is seemingly insignificant. Meg and Claire encapsulate this by talking about making allowances for others and abstaining from acting in a way that could aggravate the situation. Clearly, constantly having to tiptoe around a perpetually moody flatmate is not appropriate and will eventually take its toll on the household. "Consideration" is a term that frequently surfaced in the talk about preventing conflict. Tamsin suggests that consideration for others improves with sharing: another positive aspect of the lifestyle. Consideration and proficient interpretation of emotions promote harmony, reducing the likelihood of conflict.

A second part of the avoidance aspect of managing conflict is to brush aside problems and attempt to ignore any discord. Confrontation for the conflict-averse, even in an agreeable way, can be extremely stressful. Tough conversations mean moving out of comfort zones. Many shy away from dealing with issues for fear of damaging relationships and to maintain harmony. Thirty-two-year-old Maree justifies avoidance of addressing problems:

I'm more likely to just try
and skirt around them

than address them directly
sometimes they resolve themselves
because people move out
because flatting is not always a permanent situation
so sometimes you might put up with things
because it's only going to last
x number of months more
or you know someone's on their way out
so you might just let some things slide

The idiom "skirt around" conveys avoidance. "Sometimes they resolve themselves" could refer to the possibility of someone moving out but could also be explained by tension diminishing with time. Given the often transient nature of flatting, the chances of the source of the problem moving out are good. Avoiding confrontation is sensible if someone is about to leave. In addition, a person who knows they are departing is less likely to be cooperative if confronted. By adopting a passive approach and long-term perspective many sources of conflict resolve themselves if one is patient.

Avoiding conflict could be considered a negative coping strategy but it can serve as a necessary stress reduction function.[10] Preventing tension by sensitivity to moods and avoiding ways of communicating that create unnecessary friction is a positive approach, provided the practice is mutual. Circumventing contentious issues, motivated by aversion to confrontation and/or the transitional nature of flatting, may not always be negative and is a means of maintaining relationships.[11] If a problematic flatmate is leaving it's best to trade short-term discomfort for possible negative fallout.

Nevertheless, continuous avoidance of recurring provocation and neglecting to deal with problems can be dysfunctional. Tolerating the unacceptable means less chance of widening experience in dealing with interpersonal problems. Unresolved conflict can increase stress and distrust and become increasingly destructive if the problem is persistent and not addressed.[12] Failure to express dissatisfaction can corrode relationships and result in disengagement from communal socialising. Since household interaction is the glue that bonds households, withdrawal from socialising means the odds of continued co-residence under tense circumstances are not favourable.

An extensive analysis of over 100 group studies identified three types of group conflict.[13] Relationship conflict, which involves perceived incompatibility in personality, norms and values, is destructive if ongoing. This type of conflict can threaten self-image, increase anxiety, negative feelings and hostility as well as decrease trust.[14] Resolving relationship conflict has a relatively high probability of failure since it is emotionally charged rather than rational. Often accompanied by personal attacks such conflict inevitably results in an absence of communication. Outcomes for dealing with conflict are more positive if the group has similar values, with high levels of trust and respect.[15] As we have previously identified, young adults invariably choose to share with others very similar to themselves. And in talking about conflict, it is evident that sharers are acutely aware of what might compromise successful domestic relationships and actively seek to pre-empt potential problems by careful selection of flatmates.

Task conflict is the second type of group conflict. Task-driven conflict, such as failing to contribute to housework, frequently becomes emotion-driven adding to tension and making problem resolution difficult. This tension can be managed by focusing on overcoming individual differences to achieve a common objective. This approach is evident in housemates tackling housework together.

The third type of conflict, process conflict, has a consistently negative effect and is very likely to sabotage group viability. For example, a flatmate may consider certain tasks, such as cleaning the toilet, beneath his/her dignity.[16] Arguably, this kind of conflict can be avoided by choosing to share with people with similar expectations, values and cultures. Constraining gender roles, such as men taking out the garbage and women being responsible for cleaning the shower, are still prevalent and more acceptable in some cultures but not likely to be welcomed in egalitarian shared households.

While the two methods of managing conflict appear somewhat counterintuitive, both have the common goal of dealing with tensions detrimental to harmonious domesticity. Openly discussing problems is active and direct, while avoidance is passive, subtle and indirect. Depending on the context, different tactics need to be adopted at different times with sound, compassionate conflict management skills requiring the ability to be both confronting and avoidant.[17] The skill lies in discerning which tactic is appropriate. Both strategies acknowledge the consequences of escalating tension for the well-being of the group and continued household survival.

Consequences of conflict

Two commonly occurring discourses arose when discussing the consequences of unresolved conflict: negative psychological states and moving out. Conflict avoidance can have negative psychological implications, as explained by student Justin.

> *If there's something that*
> *really frustrates you about living with people*
> *and it's never brought up*
> *and you don't communicate properly*
> *it can be really bad*
> *it can be like you're always in a bad mood*
> *and that sort of thing but then as soon as*
> *the conflict is resolved it like levels out*
> *it's sort of another layer of things*
> *to keep on top of*
> *to keep yourself feeling good*
> *if you don't like where you're living*
> *it's bad it's not good*

Failing to deal with problems can be dysfunctional and destructive for household relationships, compromising a positive outlook on life. Not acknowledging or communicating problems can be frustrating and adversely impact moods and morale. Again, sound communication is stressed as essential in constructively solving problems. Once the conflict is settled tension abates. Elevated stress levels due to household tension, in addition to everyday pressures, are evident in Justin's open admission of trying to cope with life. Young adulthood is an exciting period of possibilities but also a turbulent life stage with multiple challenges, such as resisting peer pressure, gaining qualifications, making career choices and forming early sexual relationships.[18] Although conflict can be reversed through effective resolution, non-resolution can produce negative outcomes, with detrimental psychological and physiological ramifications.[19] Homes should be an important refuge and not compound day-to-day demands.

The dominant consequence of unsettled differences or perpetual conflict or tension is to move out, ask the perceived offender to depart or create a new household without the unsuitable housemate. According to counsellor Sam, one benefit of flatting is the ability to move out when conflict or relationships become unbearable.

I guess one advantage of flatting
is that if things do get too bad
you'll just say, "Well I'll move out,"
and you can walk away from
whatever arrangement you have

While moving may not be as traumatic as divorce or dissolving a partnership with combined finances, relocating is not unproblematic. Tenancy conditions need to be adhered to and the onus of finding a replacement flatmate, acceptable to other residents, often falls to the person leaving. If the person departing the household is the leaseholder, the situation can become complex for all. With current competitive rental markets new accommodation may be difficult to find, with no guarantee that the new household will be any better. Moving can be costly, financially and emotionally. Emotionally there is a potential loss of social capital and increased anxiety with respect to fitting into a new household. Financially, extra money is required for rent in advance, bond money and moving costs. These costs highlight the importance of managing conflict before it escalates into the untenable. However, the negative psychological consequences of remaining in an uncomfortable household frequently can make moving out the most attractive option.

Carefully choosing flatmates with similar backgrounds, values and expectations can reduce the potential for tension but this considered approach can be sabotaged by the necessity of immediately finding someone to cover expenses. In addition, even with the best of intentions, it is difficult to predict how relationships will work when sharing a household. Managing tension by means of mature discussion and resolution rather than moving to another flat is the healthy approach, but leaving a tense or uncomfortable household is often regarded as the only solution to problems.

Over-controlling or too fastidious flatmates can cause tension. The following email was sent to a departing housemate, who could no longer live with the unreasonable constraints placed on her by the leaseholding flatmate.

Hi Sandy,

Just checking in as promised with a moving out checklist – there may be one or two more things to add but will keep you in the loop.

1) Please clean your room thoroughly including vacuuming and wiping skirting boards, light switches, door handles and any marks on the door/wall that can come off. Please clear the balcony drains/gutters of leaves. Please don't leave any plants, rubbish or anything that didn't come with the flat, on the balconies or in rooms or in cupboards.
2) Could you let me know if anything is damaged/broken so I can repair it asap – this includes if any light bulbs have blown in your room, the bathroom and if you could let me know about the upstairs hall and stairwell that would be great.
3) Remember with moving that the balconies are out of use.
4) After you move out I will ask the owners if they would like to check the room prior to bond refund – unlikely in this case but I will give them the option. After the owners have confirmed they are happy I can then refund your (bond) which was two weeks' rent (no expenses). For you this was $425 as it was for the old room.
5) Could you please confirm your bank details so that I don't make any errors on the transfer of your bond.
6) Remember to clear forgotten spaces – garage, cupboard under the stairs, hot water cupboard, laundry shelves and cupboard and the freezer/fridge/food cupboard!
7) Please wipe clean all cupboards, drawers including the bathroom, the Tupperware drawer or any spaces where you had things stored.
8) Please leave any cleaning products or anything that was purchased by the flat, i.e. chopping board/knives/tea towels and hand towels (laundered would be great, please and thank you).
9) Please leave anything that came with the flat, i.e. laundry racks, shoe racks and mirrors.
10) Please leave your key on the kitchen bench when you have finished your final clean.
11) Please ensure you change your address for all mail you expect to receive, this would be greatly appreciated as it creates a lot of extra admin.

While this type of attention to detail may be efficient and in keeping with the landlord's requirements, it can be the final insult to someone moving out because of an over-controlling flatmate.

Evaluating whether the behaviour is considered appropriate, wrong or inconsiderate is often dictated by cultural and personal values.[20] Consequently, what is considered acceptable in one flat may not be so in another. The necessity for flatmates to have similar expectations in a number of spheres was commonly drawn on when talking of desirable flatmates. Clearly, tension and stress can arise from imbalances.

An important factor when considering conflict in shared housing is that there are few guiding ideological blueprints. Basic rules such as respecting others' privacy and possessions do apply, and breaching these do have consequences. In the egalitarianism of flatting traditional cultural hierarchies and socially defined gender roles are lacking. Gendered identities embedded in marital ideologies are disrupted. The well-established expectations of interactions between members of nuclear families do provide some sense of stability for relationships: potential conflicts and disagreements may be lessened and make relationships easier to sustain. Kirsten Natalier argues that shared households create their own lifestyles with countercultural values, alternative to those of the established culture, and these are used to understand and manage relationships.[21] Flatting rules are seldom written or prescribed but rather evolve naturally and differ from one household to another. If everyone is in agreement on how the household should be run harmony is possible. Flatmates shape their own protocols, which are driven by the pivotal need for a workable living arrangement.

An advantage of listening to what people have to say about their experiences is that issues that may not have been considered are raised. One such factor is the impact of physical buildings, built for nuclear families, on relationship dynamics.

Can the physical building contribute to the success or failure of a shared residence?

Conflicting positions are evident in this component of shared living. Student Greg observes the effect of the building on household relationships.

We have a flat that
doesn't have a very big living room
but pretty big rooms
so we were encouraged by the flat
to stay in our rooms

In a group of five housemates, in-house socialising is limited by the communal living room being too small to accommodate them all comfortably. Given the frequent emphasis placed on social interaction among housemates, this is an important consideration. The physical limitations influence the social dynamic with private bedrooms providing more attractive spaces.

Mary stipulates some conditions about the state of the house after which the housemates become all important.

It's the people that are the most important thing
and really when it comes down to it
if the house isn't grotty

and if the room isn't a cupboard
then it's all down to the flatmates

Although the disposition of housemates ultimately defines a successful household, there are limitations to what is acceptable in housing. The colloquial "grotty" implies unacceptable standards, such as faulty plumbing, inadequate heating and mould. Likewise, a bedroom being "a cupboard" is used to describe a private domain too small for comfort. Sub-par housing is clearly undesirable and to be avoided if possible. Those who have flatted for some years report developing an experienced eye for what is acceptable in a building or not. This supports the argument that physical building is important and can impact both physiological and psychological health.

Others, like Phoebe, believe that functional dynamics are symptomatic of good housemates irrespective of the building.

The house can be falling down
but if your other housemates are fun to live with
then you can kind of look past it
which you need to be able to do
in (city suburb) *because all the houses are falling down*

Living in a house in a state of disrepair can almost be overlooked if flatmates are convivial. Flatmates associated with fun are particularly desirable. Being able to ignore the condition of a house is a prerequisite in this inner-city suburb popular with students and impecunious flatters since the housing stock is not generally well maintained. Phoebe's equanimity suggests that despite the state of the house causing some concern it is mitigated by others in the suburb being subject to the same less than satisfactory housing.

Lisa feels the building in which she once flatted impaired the dynamic in a sinister way. What began as a household who worked together to better their environment degenerated into Lisa questioning her sanity.

I don't know if it was anything to do with that place
I don't believe it's haunted, don't get me wrong
it was just a place that seemed to feed negativity
and in the end we all took it out on each other

While rejecting the notion of the building being haunted, the possibility that the building itself was the cause of tension among housemates is suggested. Interpersonal problems are attributed to the sensation of the place feeding a negative imprint into household relationships. Possibly this belief was instilled by a friend pointing out that the residence had bad feng shui. Nevertheless, the claim that the building was the source of negative energy does much work in placing the cause of interpersonal problems firmly on the physical environment. Blaming bad behaviour on the building's assumed adverse emanations defies rationality but does serve the purpose of rendering no one, including the speaker, culpable for deteriorating relationships. Notably, this building is an abandoned community hall divided into rooms by the landlords. The boarding used in partitioning was cheap chipboard, which "*would hold no secrets*", curtailing any sense of privacy.

With more and more housing in the private rental sector, there has been a notable decline in housing conditions despite rising rents.[22] Little accommodation is specifically built for sharing. Questionable landlords can maximise profit in many ways. For example, the lounge and dining room of traditional houses are converted into bedrooms and more tenants are crammed in, leaving them with just a kitchen to share. In one case known to us, even a passage is designated as a bedroom despite being the only access to the laundry. Such modifications can have a significant impact on household relationships. This study supports calls for raising awareness for alternative house designs suited to non-nuclear families.[23] Research clearly demonstrates that health and well-being are indeed affected by buildings.[24]

Healthy buildings and environments

Emily Anthes examines a range of built environments and asks how these might be improved for the benefit of the health and well-being of those living there. A number of institutional settings are considered, such as hospitals and prisons. The core message is that there is overwhelming evidence showing "the impact that our buildings can have on our health, behaviour and happiness. They shape our sleep patterns and stress levels; our diets and moods; and our physical fitness, job performance, immune responses, and social interactions".[25]

While this work speaks to the unquestioned importance of the built environment, it says little about the last of these considerations: the social interactions which take place inside the buildings which house us for most of our lives. The idea of healthy buildings is also the focus of Allen and Macomber,[26] who emphasise the point that in an evolutionary sense, our species has moved from living predominantly outdoors to now spending an estimated 90% of our time indoors. Again this points to the importance of the built environment meeting our fundamental needs of protection from the weather, which means an environment which is, at a minimum, warm and dry. Of course, there are more complex nuanced needs that arise when we share internal environments with others.

As social psychologists, we are acutely aware of the importance of the built environment on health, well-being and social interactions. And it is these interactions which are of particular interest as they have been appropriated by the dynamics of shared living. Remember, this style of living involves sharing with non-kin others and involves a necessary degree of domestic intimacy, interpersonal psychology and social interaction.

LIVING AWAY FROM EARTH

In addition to looking at how a range of built environments may be tailored to enhance health, well-being and happiness, Anthes[27] also discusses the futuristic possibility of living away from earth. Research in this area follows from what we currently know about the lives of, for example, sailors, submariners and astronauts. These people live in unusual environments while undertaking lengthy sailing trips, working on off-shore oil drilling rigs and travelling vast distances through outer space. While these environments may be considered unnatural and transient, adapting successfully has some similarities with any group of individuals required to share living space. Hence, it can be argued that isolated and confined environments provide an intensified version of what may take place with any group living together. Indeed, Lawrence Palinkas[28] suggests such environments can be regarded as natural laboratories for the study of human social interactions.

Astronauts must live in extremely confined spaces with colleagues, who they may not know that well. Working and living alongside others in confined quarters can produce inescapable stress. In space, or while wintering in the Antarctic, it's not possible to de-stress by taking a calming walk to a nearby park. This is the reason space agencies aim to select compatible teams, however, interpersonal tension can still arise.

Simulating life on Mars

The promise of simulations is they can provide insight into issues which can be anticipated and, when problematic, perhaps minimised or even avoided. In 2015, six crew (half male and half female) entered a simulated environment for a 12-month stay. The environment was a sealed two-storey geodesic dome located on the side of a volcano in Hawaii, and it aimed to simulate life on Mars. Sandra Häuplik-Meusburger and colleagues[29] ensured the crew acted as if on Mars with strict daily routines, wearing space suits when they left the dome and having no face-to-face contact with anyone outside the dome. The researchers reported tensions and social rifts, which only became exacerbated as time went on. Activities involving all six crew members were either forced or avoided. Group dinners became tense and as the "mission" unfolded individuals increasingly sought the privacy of their own bedrooms.

In studying the effects of extreme environments, researchers in Antarctic psychology (e.g. Palinkas)[30] have noted two important but contrasting effects. Firstly, greater social cohesion can be experienced due to members of the group undergoing the commonality of isolation, confinement and extreme weather conditions. Secondly, within these environments it has been consistently documented that the greatest source of stress is due to interpersonal conflict and tension. Unchecked, such tensions can have catastrophic consequences, as a 2018 report in the Daily Mail illustrates. A Russian scientist, Sergey Savitsky, stabbed a colleague, Oleg Beloguzov, at an Antarctic research station.[31] Both men were avid readers and Beloguzov provoked Savitsky by repeatedly telling him the endings of books he was reading. This provocation eventually saw Savitsky plunge a kitchen knife into Beloguzov's chest resulting in him being evacuated to an intensive care unit in a Chilean hospital. The attacker was deported to St Petersburg where he was arrested. The incident was apparently fuelled by alcohol and the "tiny" shared living space.

While such violent outbursts are fortunately rare Sara Wheeler reports a personal relationship breakdown in 1959 when a Soviet scientist killed a colleague with an ice axe following a dispute over a game of chess.[32] The Soviets have since banned chess at their Antarctic stations. While these brutal incidents highlight what can happen when conflict escalates, it is important to keep this in perspective. High levels of hostility, even in extreme environments, are almost always managed without physical violence.

This highlights the importance of tolerating the oddities and idiosyncrasies of those we share with. And, as Emma Barrett and Paul Martin note, this is a two-way street where we need to tolerate others and also make ourselves tolerable.[33] This can mean rising above petty irritations regarding the habits of others and making sure our own habits slide under the annoyance radar of our flatmates. Unlike those trapped on the ice, we do mostly have the ability to diffuse friction in the home by escaping even during the Covid lockdown in many countries. As mentioned, a short walk to a park or even a brief retreat to the seclusion of one's bedroom may be all that is required to calm simmering tensions.

Conclusion

While many positive advantages, both economic and social, can be gained from living with peers, interpersonal relationships can be challenging. Clearly, participants had experienced household tension or conflict but tried to ensure it was minimally unsettling to their generally positive assessment of shared living. Nevertheless, the decision to move out is sometimes regarded as the only viable solution. With no defined ideological templates for co-residence rules and norms evolve according to needs. And this underscores the fact that conflict management is implemented in a lifestyle where arrangements are often inexact and transitory. This can add to the uncertainty and ambiguity involved in dealing with conflict.

In addition, most housing is built for nuclear families with little purpose built for sharing, and this factor needs to be taken into account when examining interpersonal relationships and conflict.

By focusing on tensions and conflict and extremely negative experiences, as many media reports and internet sites do, a comprehensive picture of sharing is not drawn. Our research endorses Sue Heath and colleagues' assertion that house sharers are typically happy and content.[34] Flats are homes in which to unwind and enjoy the support and ready-made social life available, not merely regarded as a roof overhead. By carefully negotiating the potential pitfalls of shared living, in active and passive ways, the detrimental effects of conflict on well-being can be circumvented.

Notes

1 This chapter draws on work published by the authors in the *New Zealand Journal of Psychology*: Vicky Clark, Keith Tuffin and Natilene Bowker, "Managing Conflict in Shared Housing for Young Adults," *New Zealand Journal of Psychology* 49, no. 1 (2020): 4–13.
2 George L. Kelling and James Q. Wilson, "Broken Windows: The Police and Neighborhood Safety," *The Atlantic Monthly* 249 (1982): 29–38, http://www.theatlantic.com/magazine/archive/1982/03/broken-windows/304465.
3 Frances Baum, "Shared Housing: Making Alternative Lifestyles Work," *Australian Journal of Social Issues* 24 (1986): 197–212; Sue Heath and Elizabeth Cleaver, *Young, Free and Single? Twenty-Somethings and Household Change* (Hampshire: Palgrave Macmillan, 2003).
4 Brian H. Spitzberg and William R. Cupach, "Disentangling the Dark Side of Interpersonal Communication," in *The Dark Side of Interpersonal Communication*, 2nd ed., eds Brian H. Spitzberg and William R. Cupach (Mahwah, NJ: Lawrence Erlbaum Associates, 2007), 3–28.
5 Morton Deutsch, "Cooperation, Competition and Conflict," in *The Handbook of Conflict Resolution: Theory and Practice*, 3rd ed., eds Peter T. Coleman, Morton Deutsch and Eric C. Marcus (San Francisco, CA: John Wiley & Sons, 2014), 3–28.
6 Frances Baum, "Shared Housing."
7 Ginka Toegel and Jean-Louis Barsoux, "How to Preempt Team Conflict," *Harvard Business Review* 94 (2016): 78–83.
8 Deutsch, "Cooperation, Competition and Conflict."
9 Jinseok S. Chun and Jin Nam Choi, "Members' Needs, Intragroup Conflict, and Group Performance," *Journal of Applied Psychology* 99, no. 3 (2014): 437–450; Petru L. Curşeu, Smaranda Boroş and Leon A. G. Oerlemans, "Task and Relationship Conflict in Short-Term and Long-Term Groups: The Critical Role of Emotion Regulation," *International Journal of Conflict Management* 23 (2012): 97–107.
10 Sheldon Cohen, "Social Relationships and Health," *American Psychologist* 59 (2004): 676–684.
11 Tamara Afifi, John Caughlin and Walid Afifi, "The Dark Side (and Light Side) of Avoidance and Secrets," in *The Dark Side of Interpersonal Communication*, 2nd ed., eds Brian H. Spitzberg and William R. Cupach (Mahwah, NJ: Lawrence Erlbaum Associates, 2007), 61–92.
12 Spitzberg and Cupach, "Disentangling the Dark Side."
13 Frank R. C. de Wit, Lindred L. Greer and Karen A. Jehn, "The Paradox of Intragroup Conflict: A Meta-analysis," *Journal of Applied Psychology* 97 (2012): 360–390.
14 Toegel and Barsoux, "How to Preempt Team Conflict."
15 Karen A. Jehn and Elizabeth A. Mannix, "The Dynamic Nature of Conflict: A Longitudinal Study of Intragroup Conflict and Group Performance," *Academy of Management Journal* 44 (2001): 238–251.
16 De Wit, Greer and Jehn, "The Paradox of Intragroup Conflict."
17 Michael E. Roloff and Danette E. Ifert, "Conflict Management through Avoidance: Withholding Complaints, Suppressing Arguments, and Declaring Topics Taboo," in

Balancing the Secrets of Private Disclosures, ed Sandra Petronio (Mahwah, NJ: Lawrence Erlbaum Associates, 2000), 151–179.

18 Jeffrey Jenson Arnett, *Emerging Adulthood: A Theory of Adulthood From the Late Teens through the Twenties*, 2nd ed. (New York: Oxford University Press, 2015).

19 Cohen, "Social Relationships and Health."

20 Raymond B. Chiu and Rick D. Hackett, "The Assessment of Individual Moral Goodness," *Personal Relationships* 26 (2017): 31–46.

21 Kristen Natalier, "I'm Not His Wife": Doing Gender in Share Households," Unpublished Doctoral Thesis. University of Queensland, 2003.

22 Elinor Wilkinson and Ilana Ortega-Alcázar, "Stranger Danger? The Intersectional Impacts of Shared Housing on Young People's Health & Wellbeing," *Health & Place* 60 (2019): 102–191.

23 Gill Jones, "Experimenting with Households and Inventing Homes," *International Social Science Journal* 164 (2000): 183–194; Andrew Beer and Debbie Faulkner, *Housing Transitions Through the Life Course; Aspirations, Needs and Policy* (Bristol: Policy Press, 2011).

24 Emily Anthes, *The Great Indoors: The Surprising Science of How Buildings Shape Our Behaviour, Health and Happiness* (New York: Scientific American, 2020).

25 Anthes, *The Great Indoors*, 209.

26 Joseph Allen and John Macomber, *Healthy Buildings: How Indoor Spaces Drive Performance and Productivity* (Cambridge, MA: Harvard University Press, 2020).

27 Anthes, *The Great Indoors*.

28 Lawrence A. Palinkas, "The Psychology of Isolated and Confined Environments: Understanding Human Behavior in Antarctica," *American Psychologist* 58, no. 5 (2003): 353–363.

29 Sandra Häuplik-Meusburger, Kim Binsted and Tristan Bassingthwaighte, "Habitability Studies and Full Scale Simulation Research: Preliminary Themes Following HISEAS Mission IV." Paper Presented at 47th International Conference on Environmental Systems, Charlestown, Carolina, July 16–20, 2017.

30 Palinkas, "The Psychology of Isolated and Confined Environments."

31 Will Stewart, "Russian Scientist 'Tried to Kill' a Colleague at Antarctic Research Station 'Because the Man Kept Giving Away the Endings of Books He Was Reading'," *Daily Mail Australia Online*, October 30, 2018, www.dailymail.co.uk/news/article-6332895/Scientist-tried-kill-colleague-kept-giving-away-endings-books-reading.html.

32 Sara Wheeler, *Terra Incognita: Travels in Antarctica* (New York: Modern Library, Random House, 2014).

33 Emma Barrett and Paul Martin, *Extreme: Why Some People Thrive at the Limits* (Oxford: Oxford University Press, 2014).

34 Sue Heath, Katherine Davies, Gemma Edwards and Rachel M. Scicluna, *Shared Housing, Shared Lives: Everyday Experiences Across the Lifecourse* (London: Routledge, 2019).

7

THE SOCIAL DYNAMICS OF SHARING

The previous chapter explored the causes, management and consequences of conflict in shared living. While household chores have been identified as the prime source of conflict, this is not the only issue over which flatmates can fall out. These include economic tensions, freeloading and different approaches to cleanliness and tidiness. We also considered the potential for the physical building to impact interpersonal household dynamics.

We begin the chapter by including topics which arose in talks about flatting but were not dominant, such as the enjoyment of communal meals. These can contribute to or detract from successful dynamics. We end the chapter with two further considerations that could affect domestic relationships: household numbers and uneven power balance.

Cooking together or independently?

Brigida Marovelli notes that the practice of eating together is an important human ritual with positive psychological benefits beyond the biological need for food. Scholars of food studies have demonstrated that sharing meals creates solidarity, bonds members and creates a sense of common identity.[1] According to Rebecca Williamson, sharing food both shapes and is shaped by social relationships in domestic environments. She examined the importance of the day-to-day food arrangements in New Zealand flat households in creating, maintaining or disintegrating social relationships through the various tasks of shopping for food, cooking and meal sharing. Through this, she identified a fundamental tension between the assertion of individuality and sociability within the flat environment.[2] This is consistent with our finding that a good flatmate understands the fine balance between being sufficiently sociable but also an independent individual.

DOI: 10.4324/9781003161370-7

Although food arrangements vary our findings suggest that in the first year of flatting shared cooking is common but in time individuals tend to opt to shop for and prepare their own meals. In addition, town folk were more likely to dine together on a daily basis but this was not as prevalent in cities.

Two town-based builders have a working ad hoc arrangement:

Ben: *Whoever's home first*
we just cook for both of us

Both Ben and flatmate Jeff, like many New Zealanders, are keen hunters of wild stag and boar so presumably have very similar palates. In some flats different dietary preferences and requirements can complicate communal cooking. Twenty-nine-year-old post-doctoral researcher Amber, in reflecting on her first year of flatting, speaks of the diversity of diets which add to the complexity of cooking for the entire flat:

It was kind of fun
because we lived in a flat
with one vegan
one person who was allergic to cheese
myself a vegetarian
and Gerry who didn't eat beef
on certain nights
and then Eric who was a carnivore

City flatters are more likely to accept different diets due to convictions, religious or otherwise, allergies and different schedules leading to the practicality of preparing one's own meals. Student Jody enjoys cooking with one flatmate when both are home for the evening, but two other flatmates follow specific diets.

Two of my flatmates are very into going to the gym
so they have to have so many calories
with chicken and pasta and stuff
for muscle development
and so they do their own meals

A further point to be considered is differences in disposable incomes. Some students may be very well supported by parents while others may not. Postgraduate students preferring to share with peers of similar age rather than undergraduates may also have to manage their money more carefully than fully employed flatmates. Recently graduated city dweller Sean explains how differences in budgets or cultures can impact cooking arrangements. Earlier, Sean had mentioned that his flatmates had emigrated to New Zealand as children from various countries but were suitably acculturated to the Kiwi way of life.

There was no kind of interaction
as far as cooking with each other
because we had a very wide range of cultures
different cultures different foods
and also different budgets as well
myself I am quite thrifty
I call myself Spartan
I eat in order to survive and
other people had larger food budgets
or preferred having different kinds of interesting food
so we all bought of our own food

Research indicates that while dietary assimilation of host country cuisine is common, immigrants generally prefer to maintain their original food culture. Consequently, most immigrants tend to develop bicultural eating patterns. Young adults, having grown up in immigrant households, may associate food from their childhoods with warm feelings and good memories. Such food often becomes comfort food, particularly in times of frustration and stress.[3]

Thirty-two-year-old seasoned flatter Julie has lived through various flat food arrangements but sees the positive side of cooking for each other.

Now I only live with one other person
we buy our own food
but I'll cook one night a week
and she'll cook one night a week
and then usually we might go out for dinner one night
and then one week I might cook twice
and she might cook twice the next week
so it evens out. I hate cooking
so it's just nice even if someone just makes
baked beans on toast I love it
cause I don't have to do it

Sharing cooking duties means that sometimes, even when the food is mundane, housemates get the benefit of having a meal cooked for them: yet another positive benefit of sharing. Those who did have cooking rosters spoke of the importance of flexibility in arrangements and this extract clearly indicates that this approach works, providing there is reciprocity.

Even in flats where everyone fends for themselves food-wise, there are times when meals are shared on an impromptu basis. Project manager Lucy speaks of living in a particularly enjoyable household:

Everyone has different eating requirements
we all do our own thing

you're not home at the same time
to eat together and then there would be the odd
Sunday or Wednesday night
where it's like, "I'm going to make
macaroni cheese. Who wants in.
Cool you bring some wine.
You bring bread, and you make a salad".
Game on, organised . . .
for me if it's one person
(it's) *omelette and some veggies*
sweet, eat it, go
but if there is another person
or two other people in the mix as well
I'll make a bit of an effort
and end up with some good meals

The fun and enjoyment of spontaneous and convenient communal eating when everyone contributes in a collective way is apparent. In her present flat, Lucy speaks of adding more rituals to their lives like watching certain TV programmes together, one of which prompted a flat cooking competition.

We did do a 'Come Dine with Me'
which was really fun, really cool
I think everyone got pretty excited
because you had to cook for six people
we had some amazing meals
and that's what's nice about
being able to cook for other people

There are positive benefits for all concerned with the fun of cooking for others and also having others cook for you. Such fun challenges, resulting in communal meals, have the potential to help build good relations among members of a flat. One household of two mature flatmates, in their mid-thirties, invite friends over to participate in making meals in which they celebrate a traditional dish from a particular country. Polish pierogies are but one example.

Postgraduate student Pia spoke of opting out of communal food arrangements because of having to adhere to the dietary requirements of fellow flatmates and also gaining weight. But she too stresses the sociability of occasional communal meals, enhancing connections.

We did like to do things together
like we would have the occasional
I guess kind of family meal
which I really enjoyed

I don't know how to describe it
a really nice social occasion
it's like a different kind of interaction
when you sit down and share a meal with someone
actually doing something special

The enjoyment of shared meals among housemates is evident and the lack of frequency adds to the special nature of the occasion. Claudia Giacoman regards both exceptional and everyday eating together as interactional, an act of communication between participants. Pia may struggle to articulate this but clearly understands that sharing meals is a form of communication.[4] Physiotherapist Susie sees the positives of both preparing and sharing food.

I think communal cooking makes you a family
I suppose food is always quite important . . .
whenever you share the shopping
and you share food
that makes you a real kind of
warm family

Susie relates food sharing to creating a "family". Other participants commonly drew on the familial aspect of sharing a roof overhead.

The flat as family

Twenty-five-year-old chef Max states, "*I view flatmates as being family that you choose*". This endorses early findings by Charles Despres that functional shared accommodation operates as a surrogate "family of choice", providing a sanctuary of companionship, support and security with strong social and emotional attachments.[5] Similarly, Counsellor Sam notes:

It's a family arrangement
once you're living in shared spaces
we got to know each other really well
and we had a quite a close knit family

The "close knit family" continues to meet by way of monthly book group discussions. This is not limited to the flat members themselves but also includes the extended network of friends gained while flatting together. The extended "family" not only shares common links by having lived together and gained mutual friends but also shares a love of reading books.

Student Jody, who flats with three guys, regards her flatmates as brothers.

So our dynamic's kind of like siblings
we take the piss out of each other
and the boys play fight

Successful flats are frequently conflated with home and family. Family prototypes of traditional nuclear families are often employed analogically to describe relationships; for example, "flat mother" or "matriarch" are terms used to indicate housemates who are particularly caring or controlling. One close-knit all-women flat referred to a housemate as resembling a camp mother. In addition to taking on financial responsibility, she was very circumspect in ascertaining why someone had not come home for the night. This demonstrates the level of care associated with families. While no one is prepared to take on a parental role to nag housemates about failure to do chores, some do take on leadership roles by making sure bills are paid on time and reminding others when payments are due. This is often by way of a social media platform, such as Facebook. In a similar vein, flatmates were sometimes described as brothers or sisters with attendant sibling teasing or squabbling, suggesting differences but familial acceptance and mutual affection.

Policeman Mike regards himself as "father" of the flat but qualified this by referring to himself as the "house leader". Mike believes in the importance of feeling part of a family environment in a shared household.

> *Well I think that's probably*
> *the biggest thing in a flat*
> *to have a good environment*
> *is to have that sort of family feel*

Only one participant spoke of her flat as merely a place to sleep despite speaking positively about her flatmates. Many regarded their flats as homes or family. Household pets are often associated with families. Do they have a role in shared accommodation?

Furry flatmates

While the topic of pets was not pervasive, there are those who associate pets with a feeling of "home". The resident cat, belonging to Meg, in a flat of all-women was a popular household member.

Annie: *She's a huge part of the flat dynamic*
I feel like she has made it feel like a home
Meg: *She's got the biggest personality*

One flat of three young working women had a German Shepherd, which they took turns to exercise. As the area they lived in was fairly rough, the dog gave them some sense of protection. Nevertheless, pets can also be a source of tension. Chef Max speaks of a perpetually unemployed flatmate who was not only unable to meet her expenses but also neglected her cat.

> *She couldn't support her cat*
> *she didn't clean up after it*

and it wasn't that well litter trained
so those kind of things really did egg me

Pets are expensive to maintain and do require a certain amount of care. Fellow flatmates may resent feeling obliged to take on responsibilities for a flatmate's pet.

Emma Power suggests that companion animals may constitute a form of escalating risk through the choice to keep pets without the landlord's knowledge. This is due to the low availability of pet-friendly rental accommodation.[6] Project manager Michelle had an experience where two flatmates brought home two kittens when pets were forbidden by the landlord. In addition, the cats did some damage.

I just couldn't understand
because we weren't allowed pets
I find it pretty stressful
if someone is not following those (rules)
because I don't want it to come back on me

A negative consequence of disregarding rules is the possibility of losing bond money. This is paid on moving into a flat in case of any damage to the property. Since everyone contributes to the bond, the loss is felt by everyone. Maree adds a further problem with not adhering to requirements:

It's about protecting your reputation as a tenant
sometimes landlords ask for references
so to avoid being blacklisted
you rely on your flatmates to be responsible as well

These are valid concerns. According to Emma Power, there is evidence of connections between rental insecurity and poor animal welfare outcomes. Housing and rental access are recognised as key factors motivating accelerating levels of pet relinquishment in a number of studies.[7] Whereas this may or may not be accurate for flatting households they can be fairly transient establishments. Young people may choose to move overseas or travel for a considerable period of time. In that case who inherits the animal? Unless the pet owner(s) has obliging friends or family, the outcome for animals can be negative. While animals can contribute to a positive household dynamic, next we explore how young house sharers themselves define the concept of the flat "dynamic".

The flat dynamic

In our initial research on housemate selection, the imperative for new members to fit in with the flat dynamic was cited as crucial. Yet the notion of the flat dynamic was never made explicit. This led to further research in which we sought to peel back the onion to see what folk meant by this. We found that the flat dynamic was frequently regarded as synonymous with functionality and succinctly described as "how things work".

How flatting works

Student Toni interprets the flat dynamic as "*how everything fits together and works*". She uses her current flat as an example of a successful dynamic.

> *My current dynamic*
> *as I said earlier*
> *everyone gets along*
> *we understand we have to do certain things*
> *to help keep the place going*
> *cleaning, everything*
> *we all know we need to do these things*

In Toni's current flat interpersonal relationships are convivial and this is attributed to a shared and well-understood sense of important duties and responsibilities. "Cleaning" singled out as housework is most likely to be the source of conflict. Whereas "how everything fits together" evokes a picture of an interlocking jigsaw puzzle, many participants spoke of the need for "balance" for a functional household dynamic and optimal harmony.

A workable balance

Various dimensions comprise this aspect.

Balancing the social and the private

The ability to respect the fine balance between public sociability and the right to privacy and independence has previously been identified as a key requirement in an acceptable flatmate. In describing a workable dynamic, project manager Lucy draws on this discourse, emphasising that given the right blend of people flatting is fun.

> *I've had some great flatting experiences*
> *we were all quite fun people so*
> *enjoyed having people around*
> *found it social for drinks*
> *and all of our groups of friends melded together*
> *and it was really cool*
> *and we are all still friends now*
> *which is awesome*
> *but it comes down to*

I guess personality
and what works
we had the right balance of
having our own lives
and doing things that we enjoy
and then coming out being social with each other

Lucy ascribes "great flatting experiences" to commonalities with each other. She repeatedly stressed that she regards shared housing as "home" not merely a roof overhead. Positive aspects, such as fun, friendship and socialising are linked to personality and ultimately impact a workable dynamic, substantiating the functional aspects. In this case the personalities have resulted in friendships that outlived the household. The level of sociability invokes the image of one big extended group of happy young people, who lived together and enjoyed each other's company. This included compatible friends, who widened the social group. In this case the "right balance" between being sociable with housemates and also entitlement to having independent lives is evident. Lucy talks of "coming out" and being social, which we interpret as emerging from the private bedroom domain.

Thirty-four-year-old Phoebe struggles to explain why certain flats function successfully but, like Lucy, concludes that it entails the "right balance".

There were three of us
me, Robyn and Rosie
and that dynamic was perfect
it just worked so nicely
I just can't put my finger
on what it was I think it's just
the right balance of us being
sociable but also not
in each other's faces
also being independent but
also enjoying each other's company
and laid back enough to
share bottles of wine together
but then it's also OK if we just want to
sit in our rooms and close the door
and be a hermit

These two extracts are remarkably similar with both, like Toni, describing good interpersonal relationships as key components for functional flatting. Phoebe speaks of enjoying each other's company and sharing wine, which echoes Lucy's description of enjoying socialising with flatmates and their friends. Both employ the particularly pervasive observation of the necessity for a balance between public sociability and the right to independence and privacy behind closed bedroom doors. Lucy talks of socialising as "coming out". Phoebe uses the metaphor of a "hermit", which was employed by others as well, to describe times of solitude.

In the intimacy of shared housing, sociability needs to be balanced with a sense of privacy and independence. The right balance contributes to positive relationships and harmony and requires careful navigation, tact and interpersonal sensitivity to the needs of others.

Counsellor Sam also draws on personalities to construct the dynamics of flatting.

> *My previous flatmate was*
> *very very introverted*
> *and being around large groups of people*
> *for him could be quite stressful*
> *whereas I quite like to be out*
> *or have people over*
> *and it can make things more difficult*
> *but then it's also down to me*
> *and to him to understand that I can't*
> *have people over every night*
> *it's just not fair and also that*
> *I can or should be able*
> *to have people over*
> *because that's how flatting works*
> *you have to accept both sides*
> *it's about finding balance*
> *between each other's expectations*

Divergent preferences for levels of sociability can be an impediment but can be overcome by "finding balance" in expectations and a reciprocal understanding and appreciation of differing needs and fairness. This contrasts with Lucy's interpretation of having the "same expectations". When expectations align accommodating the needs of others diminishes but when differences exist harmony can be achieved through a delicate balance of compromise, negotiation, and give and take. "Because that's how flatting works" is a categorical statement about accepting differences and finding a workable balance.

Balance between excessively tidy or messy

Another dimension of shared living that requires careful balancing is a mutually acceptable standard of cleanliness and tidiness.

Builders Jeff and Ben spoke of having similar ideas of cleanliness and tidiness.

> *Jeff: Both of us aren't messy people*
> *but we're not anal clean people either*
> *like if you had a real clean freak*

you'd feel a bit out of it
and if you lived with a real messy person
you'd tell them to clean up
Ben: I suppose it's just a balance

We know that obsessively tidy and clean flatmates are not popular and can cause tension. Jeff substantiates that the dynamic can be compromised by those whose ideals of cleanliness and tidiness are too high to live up to or too low to tolerate. "You'd feel a bit out of it" implies alienation. "Anal clean people" and "real clean freak" are pejorative suggesting abnormality and unacceptability. "Anal" has negative connotations associated with the Freudian concept of arrested development, compulsive order, tidiness, precision and perfection seeking.[8] A common understanding of the concept is assumed. "Messy" people are similarly regarded as a liability but are more easily accommodated. Jeff positions himself and Ben as well adjusted, neither messy nor obsessively clean, with Ben concluding that a balance between the two poles is optimal. Positioning others as obsessive deflects any suggestion of the speaker being less than hygienic.

Day-to-day housekeeping requires equilibrium between clean and tidy and overly demanding expectations. Frances Baum and Rebecca Williamson have observed that much hinges on individuals' interpretations of what constitutes an acceptable standard of hygiene with bathrooms and kitchens particularly contentious areas.[9] Order in one household may seem like chaos in another.

Recently graduated Sean, working in retail before taking up a scholarship overseas, also speaks of a necessary balance:

There was actually a point last year
when I thought it went a bit too far
one of our flatmates was even quite anal
on these sorts of things
started putting up notes around the house
notes on the fridge saying,
remember to shut the fridge door
notes on the cupboard and stuff
but it didn't go down very well
because again I quite like the idea
of being able to live in a flat
without being told what to do
there is an equilibrium there
I think that needs to be had

Like Jeff, Sean employs the term "anal" to refer to undesirable behaviour, taking for granted the listener's interpretation of the term. "Remember to shut the fridge door" implies a totally unwarranted and futile instruction. The three sites of the notes, "notes around the house", "notes on the fridge" and "notes on the cupboards" form a tripartite list, which is a rhetorical device used to legitimise claims by signifying a complete inventory.[10] In this case, the impression of innumerable, unnecessary notes attached to various surfaces is conveyed. Other participants regarded leaving notes as passive aggression. Sean justifies his stance by stating that he does not enjoy being told what to do. "Again" refers to an earlier statement about flatting representing freedom from the demands and rules of the parental home. Sean too concludes that there needs to be an equilibrium or balance of expectations for successful co-habitation. Functional dynamics are also contingent upon agreement about the need to consider others without being treated like mindless children, who need notes to remind them of their domestic responsibilities. Flatmates oblivious to others' time management strategies can also create tension.

Balanced routines

Shared households are often humble establishments with few luxuries, such as ensuites, and very often one bathroom is shared among multiple people. The timing of morning ablutions constitutes an important feature of workable co-habitation as noted by temp worker Phoebe:

> *It's a very delicate balance*
> *it's worked quite nicely so far*
> *because Robyn gets up first and has a shower*
> *and then I get up and have a shower*
> *and then Maia gets up and has a shower*
> *so it's quite good in that we all have*
> *very staggered morning routines*
> *that works really well*

A respected order of routine, such as staggered shower times can contribute to harmonious living. As Phoebe notes, in the weekday morning rush a balancing act of timing is required if all are to complete their ablutions satisfactorily. Flatmates failing to adhere to established routines were often a source of discontent. Student teacher Kim's dissatisfaction with a new flatmate was "*One morning she took a shower in my time*". Generally, new housemates are expected to slot into existing routines, suggesting that the egalitarianism of communal living favours long-term residents. In addition, friends staying overnight and appropriating the bathroom and hot water are vexatious and can upset the status quo.

Gender balance

A particular gender is not often a compulsory requirement in flat composition. According to counsellor Julie, if a potential flatmate is more likeable than another that takes preference over a balance of males and females:

> *It doesn't matter if they are male or female*
> *we usually try to keep it balanced*
> *because there's five of us*
> *at the moment it's three girls and two boys*

In flats of odd numbers absolute equilibrium is impossible but some modulation is achievable. While two women stated preferences for male housemates, gender of flatmates was generally regarded as irrelevant but a balance of genders was mooted as contributing to functional dynamics. However, of the seven flat groups interviewed two were all-women and two were all-men, suggesting the possibility of single-gender household preference, but this could be happenstance and tie in with the selection of the best fit with the existing dynamic.

Balance is easily destabilised

Interpersonal relationships in the intimacy of domesticity can be fragile. This is demonstrated by the recognition that two flatmates starting a relationship can destabilise the delicate balance. Call centre worker Lisa alludes to this:

> *So we started sleeping together*
> *which offset the balance again in the house*

We are not informed how the "balance" was offset by "sleeping together" but this was part of a lengthy narrative of how a seemingly successful flat dynamic rapidly deteriorated due to a number of factors. Single participants are often averse to flatting with couples due to couples not socialising sufficiently or exerting undue power by virtue of numbers: the latter could undoubtedly affect the equilibrium.

Discourses of a balance requisite in many aspects of shared households pervaded talk. Essentially, this is walking a fine line between two alternatives, evoking a metaphor of funambulism: the art of tightrope walking, where you have to lean to one side and then the other to remain balanced and avoid the hazard of falling. Kathryn Greene, Valerian Derlega and Alicia Mathews see a comparison of tightrope walking with interpersonal relationships, suggesting the need for continual maintenance and repair of tensions.[11] Living collectively in close confines on a daily basis could compound the need for constant monitoring and compromising to sustain relationships as any group can be an arena for interpersonal conflict and aggression, generating negative outcomes for members.

Human groups, like ant colonies, are not the sum of independent individuals but complex systems of interdependent characters constantly adjusting to the actions and reactions of others.[12] Consequently, it could be argued that the abstract concept of "dynamic" focuses on the holistic aspect of group interaction. Inspired by Hardin's seminal theory, the tragedy of the commons, Karsten Maus employs economic equations to demonstrate that individual rational behaviour does not function for the collective good. In the cleverly titled, The tragedy of the commune, Mause asserts that communal living may not necessarily deteriorate into tragedy but careful management is required for shared housing to function effectively.[13] Clearly, the collective good and interdependence of communal living need to be carefully balanced against self-interest if flats are to function as workable, functioning units:

an essential emotional trade-off or there are no winners. This brings us to the next closely aligned components of this discourse: each flat dynamic is unique but changeable and rarely static.

Dynamics are unique and subject to change

Mature student Claire, who lives with three other working women, observes that the dynamic of a flat evolves of its own accord without any formal structures:

I think it just sort of develops on its own
and it changes with time without anybody
putting it into place
it just sort of happens
depending on what's going on
in certain people's lives

"Putting it into place" may touch on the lack of cultural and ideological blueprints defining this way of life. Certainly, many households may start with a housework roster but find that they are not as practical as expected. Dynamics could change according to events in residents' lives. For example, "balance" can be destabilised by a change in relationships, such as two single flatmates becoming a couple. In addition, a single flatmate finding a new love interest can alter the dynamic. This could result in the flatmate going out more often and a reduction in in-house socialising or flatmates may not like the new person in their flatmate's life.

Jody interprets the flat dynamic as a function of interpersonal relationships.

I guess each flat would have a different dynamic
it's obviously very interesting
trying to find someone who fits into that dynamic

Like many participants, Jody described her present flat dynamic. Since each flat has a different dynamic, recruiting a new housemate requires finding a suitable replacement who is compatible with the dynamic. This was frequently described as the right "fit". The necessity for the right fit supports the observation that the dynamics of individual flats are unique.

According to Marie Cini, the introduction of a new person to a group can not only affect established interpersonal relationships, undoubtedly disrupt the dynamic and alter the composition of the group but can also produce positive effects.[14] Adaptation can be stressful for any newcomers to a group and longer-term members alike. A state of flux can continue until new members are assimilated and homeostasis is once again established. In addition, cohesion and commitment to the group can ebb and flow according to what is happening in an individual's life. Stresses and strains can be accommodated or initial synergy can be replaced by conflict. According to Edgar Schein, too frequent turnover of members in groups can result in a lack of inclusive culture as there is no common history.[15] Certainly, many shared households are transitory but living in close confines could accelerate social integration.

The emphasis on balance complements theoretical perspectives on group functioning, where the concept of equilibrium plays an important role. Pertinent to this study, Kurt Lewin proposed that whenever driving forces exceed restraining forces in groups, the status quo or equilibrium will change.[16] In Lewin's conception, a change in one member of a group can influence all other individuals in a group and the group as a whole. Change results in a new level of equilibrium that resists further change. Systems theory applied to groups assumes that groups maintain dynamic equilibrium among members through a complex series of adjustments and processes.[17] Social stability theory suggests groups always seek to maintain equilibrium by expelling ideas and individuals who disagree with popular opinion. This suppresses tension, helps keep society in balance and promotes harmonious co-existence. A lack of social stability can cause revolution and unrest in the group.[18] In essence, all systems tend towards some kind of equilibrium, in an attempt to reduce dissonance and promote alignment. Certainly, adjustment is required when a new individual is introduced to a household. The more successful adjust to existing conditions rather than unsettling current dynamics.

Essentially the selection process attempts to reproduce and perpetuate the existing dynamic in households currently regarded as functional and successful. A further psychological component pertains to the right fit for housemates in a cohesive, compatible whole. Again the metaphor of a jigsaw puzzle with complex interlocking pieces is apt. New arrivals are often chosen on their perceived best fit with the existing dynamic.

The right fit

A good fit was often constructed in terms of similarities across a wide spectrum among flatmates. Common assumptions in groups resulting in similar patterns of perceiving the world and behaving provide meaning, stability, comfort and reduction in anxiety[19] underscoring the emphasis participants placed on having similar expectations and values.

Julie attributes successful dynamics to selecting housemates who will fit in with the existing dynamic.

> *In my last flat there were five bedrooms*
> *so people are constantly* (changing)
> *I think I lived with 30 people*
> *over three and a half years*
> *you want to find someone*
> *who's quite similar to you*
> *someone that's going to fit into the group*
> *and when someone doesn't really fit in*
> *it's not long before they move out*

cause they get the vibe
I think if you have everyone
that's on the same page
the whole dynamic of the flat's
a lot better

Thirty people estimated to pass through a five-bedroomed flat in three and a half years amounts to a turnover of almost ten people annually. This not only accentuates the transience of this demographic but also validates Julie's experience and warrant to speak on the topic. The phrase "on the same page" or equivalents, such as "the same mindset", frequently emerged to describe ideal flatmates, suggesting that good interpersonal relationships are more likely to flourish in a climate of similar backgrounds and outlooks, including values, morals, etc. Dissimilar people are likely to move out. "Get the vibe" suggests an unsuitable person feeling uncomfortable and perhaps becoming aware of being a poor "fit". "Fit" conveys the ideal aspiration of working relationships but also the real possibility of someone falling short of the required standards: someone who does not fit. Five bedrooms would constitute a fairly large flat. Do household numbers affect the dynamic?

Some further considerations

Household numbers

The impact of the number of people living in a flat was not frequently observed. We are aware that more mature sharers prefer to flat with a maximum of two other housemates. This may suggest that experience teaches that the number in a household can impact harmony. Quite likely the financial wherewithal to share with fewer people does enter the equation.

Paul, who works in the music media industry, lives in a city mansion with 21 flatmates. Asked about the social aspects of sharing he had this to say:

Living the way we do definitely makes it a lot cheaper
but for most people it's not necessarily about that
it's more about the living environment
and being around so many interesting people
because everyone here's from quite interesting backgrounds

Despite the economic and social positives of living in a large establishment, a negative aspect is that guests are more likely to take advantage of the sheer number of householders:

There's a lot of guests coming and going
this is our home
we like people to be a little more respectful of our house
because it's such a big house too

people often think they can get away
with more than they can elsewhere

Paul, like most sharers, regards his flat as "home" and does not enjoy outsiders who have no consideration for the people who inhabit the house. If one guest can free ride and increase bills by not paying for amenities, like heating and hot water, then numerous guests could multiply the expenses.

Chef Max also spoke of the pros and cons of living in a larger household:

The large flat that I was in
if someone wanted to move out
their name wasn't on a lease
so they could just up and move
and get someone else in fill their spot . . .
Having new faces was good
because you wouldn't grow sick of someone too much
cause you would know they would be
out in a six month period
but it was also quite an isolating experience
because although we all shared common interests
and about 97% of the people who moved through that place
we all got along there was also
everyone had their own things to do
and not everyone wanted to all do something together

Some shared accommodation arrangements are not regulated through formal rental tenancy agreements meaning that not everyone is a leaseholder.[20] Being able to vacate a household without too much red tape may be regarded as a plus but leaving a household can be costly, emotionally and physically. But there are downsides to informal agreements: primarily, lack of legal protection.[21] We know that people who do not like confrontation with problematic housemates tend to hope that the offender will leave.

On the downside, Max feels that the sociability of the household can be negatively affected by too many numbers. This too may be the reason for a fast turnover of flatmates: some may be seeking closer connections within their flats. Max also mentioned that in larger flats it can be difficult to pinpoint who the messy people are but there is also an increased tendency to make one person the scapegoat for all the household problems. The question of who holds the lease leads to the discussion of uneven power relations that can arise in shared households.

Uneven power balance

In some shared housing arrangements the autonomy of an individual, within a supposedly egalitarian shared home, may be negatively impacted by unequal power relations between a sole leaseholder and subtenant. Besides lack of legal protection, if a tenant is not on the lease the leaseholder can make decisions regarding the household without the consent of flatmates.[22] Frances Baum identified two situations in which several of her participants related difficulties. The most commonly reported problem was when one flatmate owned the house. An unacceptable assumption of status and authority was also reported in long-term residents and furniture owners.[23] Project manager and veteran flatter, Maree, speaks of the detrimental side of some of these inequalities:

> *Sometimes if you've moved into*
> *an existing flat it can be hard to*
> *feel like it's your own space*
> *I moved into a flat where all of the furniture*
> *in the lounge and kitchen was*
> *owned by one of the other flatmates*
> *and it made it very hard for me to*
> *make my mark* (and) *put any of my stuff* (out)
> *because there was already stuff there*
> *so when she moved out it was actually quite nice*
> *because that was a chance to feel more like an equal . . .*
> *I think that can have an impact on*
> *how people find flatting*

The private space of a bedroom can be furnished, personalised and made comfortable with a person's possessions. Likewise, having some personal items in shared spaces can add to a sense of belonging, comfort, well-being and self-identity. Being denied this opportunity can detract from the feeling of being "home" and undermine feelings of control, security and equality. Those who rent and do not own their homes can find it difficult to make a home in a rental property but can overcome this by making a home with their personal possessions and good household relationships.[24] Feelings of precarity may be exacerbated by the often transitional nature of sharing. In addition, long-term flatmates have set the rules, which may not appeal to a newcomer. Under such conditions, a first experience of flatting can be alienating and may ultimately prejudice a person against the way of life.

Conclusion

The chapter opened and closed with factors that add to our understanding of sharing as we attempted to unravel factors important to the success or failure of shared living. The enjoyment of shared meals is evident but these occasions are often curtailed by differing timetables of housemates. The pleasure of sharing food together is linked to feeling like a family with shared households frequently regarded as home and family. Pets increase the homely feeling of flats but can also be contentious.

To date very little has been written about the dynamics of shared households among young adults: the research paradigm we employed allows for a descriptive depth to the concept of household dynamics in consultation with stakeholders. The flat dynamic was concisely defined as "how things work". We now know that for utilitarian sharing to work a fine balance is required in many areas from socialising to ablution routines. Dynamics differ from house to house and are seldom stable entities but subject to change, largely due to often itinerant populations but also day-to-day changes in inhabitants' lives. Functional households are those where people are perceived to be a good fit for each other. In essence, the flat dynamic can be defined as the property of holistic household interaction.

Finally, we briefly consider how the number of flatmates and power imbalances within the household can affect the dynamic. With larger numbers in a household frequent turnover of residents is more likely and this can be fortuitous if a housemate is unsuitable. The other side of the coin is that the greater the number of people the harder it can be to have connections and social cohesion. Uneven power balances are not conducive to egalitarianism and restrict autonomy. Both scenarios can detract from the feeling of being at home.

Notes

1 Brigida Marovelli, "Cooking and Eating Together in London: Food Sharing Initiatives as Collective Spaces of Encounter," *Geoforum* 99 (2019): 190–201.
2 Rebeccca Williamson, "Flat Food: Food, Sociability and the Individual in the New Zealand Flat," *New Zealand Sociology* 20 (2005): 4–17.
3 Tulisile Mbombo-Dweba, James Wabwire Oguttu and Christian Mbajiorg, "Factors Influencing Dietary Choices of Immigrants Upon Resettlement in Host Countries – A Scoping Review," *Applied Ecology and Environmental Research* 16, no. 2 (2018): 1329–1351.
4 Claudia Giacoman, "The Dimensions and Role of Commensality: A Theoretical Model Drawn from the Significance of Communal Eating among Adults in Santiago, Chile," *Appetite* 107 (2016): 460–470.
5 Charles Despres, "The Meaning and Experience of Shared Housing: Companionship, Security and a Home," in *Power by Design: Proceedings of the Twenty-fourth Annual Conference of Environmental Design Research Association* (Oklahoma City, OK: EDRA, 1994), 119–127.
6 Emma R. Power, "Renting With Pets: A Pathway to Housing Insecurity?," *Housing Studies* 32, no. 3 (2017): 336–360.
7 Power, "Renting With Pets."
8 Sigmund Freud, *Three Essays on the Theory of Sexuality* (Reprint, Tulsa, OK: Gardner's Books, 1991 [1905]).
9 Frances Baum, "Shared Housing: Making Alternative Lifestyles Work," *Australian Journal of Social Issues* 24 (1986): 197–212; Rebecca Williamson, "Flatting Futures."
10 Anita Pomerantz, "Extreme Case Formulations: A Way of Legitimizing Claims," *Human Studies* 9 (1986): 219–229.
11 Kathryn Greene, Valerian Derlega and Alicia Mathews, "Self-Disclosure in Personal Relationships," in *The Cambridge Handbook of Personal Relationships*, eds Anita L. Vangelisti and Daniel Perlman (Cambridge: Cambridge University Press, 2006), 409–428.
12 Donelson R. Forsyth, *Group Dynamics*, 6th ed. (Belmont: Wadsworth, 2014).
13 Garrett Hardin, "The Tragedy of the Commons," *Science* 162 (1968): 1243–1248; Karsten Mause, "The Tragedy of the Commune: Learning From Worst-Case Scenarios," *Journal of Socio-Economics* 1 (2008): 308–327.

14 Marie A. Cini, "Group Newcomers: From Disruption to Innovation," *Group Facilitation* 3 (2001): 3–13.
15 Edgar H. Schein, "Organizational Culture," *American Psychologist* 45 (1990): 109–119.
16 Kurt Lewin, "Resolving Social Conflicts and Field Theory in Social Science," *American Psychological Association* (1997), https://doi.org/10.1037/10269-000.
17 Forsyth, *Group Dynamics*.
18 Truscott Parsons, "Some Considerations on the Theory of Social Change," *Rural Sociology* 26 (1961): 219–239.
19 Schein, "Organizational Culture."
20 Sophia Maalsen and Nicole Gurran, "Finding Home Online? The Digitalization of Share Housing and the Making of Home through Absence," *Housing, Theory and Society* (2021), www.tandfonline.com/doi/abs/10.1080/14036096.2021.1986423?journalCode=
21 Nicole Gurran, Madeleine Pill, Sophia Maalsen, Tooran Alizadeh and Pranita Shrestha, *Informal Accommodation and Vulnerable Households: Scale, Drivers and Policy Responses in Metropolitan Sydney* (Sydney: Sydney Policy Lab, 2019).
22 Nicole Gurran et al., "Informal Accommodation."
23 Baum, "Shared Housing."
24 Bronwyn Bate, "Understanding the Influence Tenure Has on Meanings of Home and Homemaking Practices," *Geography Compass* 12, no. 1 (2018): e12354, https://doi.org/10.1111/gec3.12354.

8

CONCLUSION

Social psychology has long neglected important areas of social life and everyday matters, such as how people get along with each other.[1] In particular, there is a dearth of research into interactions of people in the domestic arena. Shared housing among young adults in the Western world has been a ubiquitous lifestyle for decades. Almost unheard of ten years ago, sharing among single young adults in contemporary urban Japan is now evident.[2] Research also indicates that shared housing among single young adults is also gaining popularity in South Korea.[3]

Until our research social psychologists had overlooked this way of life despite the rich opportunities for research offered in this unique microcosm of complex social systems. Scholarship has failed to understand how important sharing is in showing us about daily household practices, generational changes, patterns that mark out youth housing and the developmental changes that occur during these important years.[4]

Besides detailing the background of the lifestyle, we presented a comprehensive analysis of common discourses that emerged in the talk of our interviewees. We adopted a language-based approach to understanding the intricacies of human social life within the close confines of non-kin domesticity. Extensive extracts have been used from transcribed interviews so readers are able to decide for themselves if our interpretations of the topics discussed are well grounded.

To gain insight into the way of life we explore how folk go about finding and choosing flatmates. Rejection of potential flatmates by way of age, gender, ethnicity, mental health and substance abuse is justified by past bad experiences and the potential for a negative effect on the household dynamic. The motivation is pragmatic rather than discriminatory, with the necessity for a workable living arrangement. In examining who are regarded as desirable flatmates and why, we conclude that preferred flatmates are those similar to each other with respect to values, outlook, culture and morality. In addition, concordant expectations of each other with

DOI: 10.4324/9781003161370-8

regard to cleanliness, sociability and household guests are important. Safety, trust and the necessity for feeling comfortable in the home environment are evident in how people speak about ideal flatmates. And these prerequisites are easier to sustain by living with others similar to ourselves. Constructing ideal flatmates in terms of similarities increases understanding regarding discrimination towards dissimilar prospective flatmates. Single people tend to prefer sharing with other unattached individuals as couples are less likely to socialise and have the potential to exert unequal power. Some individuals would rather flat with friends, but friends do not always make ideal flatmates. Others prefer to flat with strangers with the potential for making new friends once ground rules are established.

There are considerable social advantages to sharing but these can be subject to sabotage by those who do not contribute fairly to household chores. Rosters are largely regarded as neither viable nor desirable ways of apportioning work and counterproductive to autonomy. If rosters are employed they need to be flexible. While housework is reported as the main source of conflict, other sources include different standards of what constitutes cleanliness, freeloading and miserliness. Good communication resulting in consensus and compromise helps circumvent problems and outright conflict. Avoiding tension by consideration, tact and sensitivity to housemates' emotional states can be preventive but avoiding discussion of issues to preserve harmony can be detrimental to household relationships. Unresolved conflict can have negative psychological and physiological consequences. Consequently, a common coping mechanism is to move out.

Other topics arising in the talk include whether to prepare and eat meals together or cook independently; the flat as a family; and furry flatmates. We look directly at participants' assessment and understanding of the all-important dynamics that structure key aspects of sharing together as well as the impact the architecture of the building lived in can have on interpersonal relationships. The topics very briefly summarised earlier are all integral to the social dynamics of shared housing and contribute to our understanding of how flats work, and how folk manage to get along within the close confines of domesticity. The topics overlap, are interconnected and intertwine to a greater or lesser degree but were separated to facilitate analysis and insight.

Recent research

Recent developments in research by sociologists, urban geographers and planners, and social policy academics testify to an increased interest and a growing volume of literature on shared housing.[5] While academics focus on different demographics, all contribute to closing significant gaps in knowledge and greater understanding of the sharing lifestyle. For example, Sophia Maalsen and Nicole Gurran found that those who do not fit the profile of an ideal flatmate, such as those with children and the underemployed, face more challenges in finding accommodation. They are subject to rental discrimination by both landlords and those seeking flatmates. Single parents and those underemployed have the potential to be more socially intrusive as they are more dependent on household space to live. Aware of these challenges, such folk stress their unobtrusiveness on digital advertising platforms for flatmates. This privileges those who do fit the ideal flatmate criteria: the young, single and childless with an active work and social life, which curtails their time spent at home and use of household space. On the plus side, digital platforms do allow those in the same circumstances, such as single mothers, part-time workers or beneficiaries to connect with each other.[6] Advertisements for new flatmates frequently include the need to be working full-time as did our participants when speaking about choosing flatmates. This speaks to the fiscal viability of flatmates who can then be relied on to pay bills and rent: a crucial, pragmatic consideration.

Sharing versus living alone

Our work is something of a counterpoint to Eric Klinenberg's 2012 book, which documents the notion of "going solo" and talks about the "extraordinary" rise in the numbers of folk living alone, and the "surprising" appeal of living solo.[7] Certainly, the number of people living alone in the USA has increased over the last 50 years, but this could reflect demographic trends such as husbands dying before their wives, increasing divorce statistics and the drop off in marriage for young people. Klinenberg attributes this trend to the rise in individualism but there are other factors at play here. The increased status of the independent woman, the growth in large metropolises and increased life expectancy are also important in understanding this trend of living alone. Klinenberg provides a tendentious account of solo living, seeing this in almost exclusively positive terms.

Arguably, Klinenberg's positivity overlooks the negative side effects that can be associated with living alone: loneliness and isolation. These psychological states arise from an absence of satisfying social relationships. While it's true that some folk prefer their own company and enjoy the peace, quiet and solitude living alone can afford, it's equally true that this lifestyle can contribute to constrained social relationships, which can serve as a prelude to loneliness. We know that loneliness is strongly linked with depression, anxiety, dissatisfaction and pessimism. And, as research (e.g. Julianne Holt-Lunstad et al.)[8] demonstrates, there is extensive evidence linking loneliness with negative health outcomes.

Vivek Murthy's 2020 book explores the importance of social connections after first making the distinction between loneliness and solitude. Solitude is referred to as voluntary isolation wherein people become comfortable with solitude and regard this as a means of strengthening connections with the self. Murthy suggests that solitude can protect against the downsides of inadequate social relationships. He discusses three dimensions of loneliness: intimate, relational and collective. The intimate may come from sharing a mutual bond of affection with a close friend; the relational stems from good friendships, companionship and social support; and the collective derives from a group sharing similar interests or purposes.[9] Our contention is that shared living can give rise to some or all of these dimensions while living solo makes them domestically unattainable.

This is particularly relevant for young adults who are one of the loneliest demographics. This is especially the case following a move to a new location for work or study, where it's possible to arrive in a new town without friends or social contacts. Solo living does not equate with loneliness, but it's clear that sharing can have an upside by providing a ready-made set of peers who, at best, can become a de facto family offering support, friendship and meaningful relationships. The psychological benefits of sharing are glaringly absent from Klinenberg's account where "the trouble with roommates" provides an impressively negative list of things that can go wrong (as noted at the beginning of Chapter 3). Living with others can be stressful and provides no guarantees for satisfying social relationships. However, our research highlights the extent to which sharing can provide an antidote to loneliness. Not all flats enjoy shared meals, fun games and relationships that develop into friendships. However, sharing provides functional relationships, which, according to Chris Masi et al., are important sources of social support and social contact that can provide a buffer against loneliness.[10] At one level sharing can help inoculate against loneliness and it can also provide a social environment which is socially and psychologically rewarding. Besides arguing for the positive side of sharing, our work both complements and contributes to extant literature and a richer understanding of this popular youthful domestic way of life.

Contribution to existing literature

The data from our research is dense and extensive and supports much of the limited extant but increasing literature on house sharing. It clearly endorses early findings that shared housing is a viable way of life, not valued solely for economic reasons and patently, environmentally responsible.[11] The social advantages outweigh the negative aspects, provided problems are dealt with intelligently and openly. However, participants strongly maintained that some individuals are not suited to the flatting lifestyle. These include the overly obsessive, controlling and those who fail to understand the necessity of mutual respect, consideration, cooperation and reciprocation.

The significant addition our work provides is that the complexity of interpersonal relationships in the domestic domain is accentuated. Nothing is clear-cut. For example, whereas Peter Kemp and Julie Rugg[12] maintain that people prefer to flat with friends, this research negates that as an immutable truth: some prefer to live with strangers. Frances Baum[13] suggests that rosters were the most effective means of dealing with household chores whereas our participants demonstrate an aversion to rosters. Less constraining systems where people have a choice are more effective. Differences in expectations of what constitutes clean and tidy highlight that excessively demanding obsessive, perfectionists can be more difficult to contend with than those less fastidious.

All observations demonstrate that the art of maintaining convivial flatting relationships is extremely complex with differing ideas as to what works and what does not. Certainly, the solution in one flat may not succeed in another. Nothing is conclusively correct or erroneous and what appeals to some may be unpalatable to others. A person who is not a good "fit" for one household may be desirable and popular in a different flat. Provided there is a general consensus as to how a household should operate, harmony can be achieved.

Talk is driven by the fundamental value associated with having a workable living arrangement. Importantly, participants are aware of the problems associated with various choices. Opinions and justifications are often based on stories of good and bad experiences, what to avoid and what has worked in the past. Hazel Christie, Moira Munro and Heidi Rettig report that sharers profit from accumulated familiarity with the way of life.[14] This is evident in long-term flatters reluctant to flat with those coming straight from the parental home. In addition, town and city flatters differ in preferences: city people are more likely to flat with strangers and less likely to eat together, while the opposite is true for townsfolk.

Our research also contributes to other areas of social psychological interest and human psychology. Matt Easterbrook and Vivian Vignoles note that group processes and dynamics may vary according to the types of groups. For example, work groups are different to social groups but little attention has been devoted to investigating different group types.[15] David Barker argues that there is a paucity of systematic investigation into behaviour dimensions in interpersonal intimacy issues in small groups.[16] Our research contributes substantial insight into small group dynamics in close confines. We now know more about the intricacies of groups of young people sharing the same domestic living space and what may contribute to the success, or otherwise, of this.

Furthermore, examining the domestic life of young adults adds considerably to comprehending transitions to adulthood in rapidly changing times. Traditional markers of adulthood, such as completion of training and education, stable employment, marriage and parenthood may be deferred with house sharing no longer a short transition gap but a much lengthier accommodation option. We agree with Jeffrey Arnett that there are new ways of understanding coming of age: house-sharing young adults are independent in different ways to previous generations and do take responsibility for their own decisions.[17] By adapting to broad political, economic and social forces they are not merely recipients but actively spearheading change.[18] Sharing, therefore, is far more significant than a simple accommodation option. Nevertheless, there is still much to be learned about the lifestyle. This brings us to further recommendations for future research to build on this work and the shortcomings of the study.

Suggested trajectories for future research

To the best of our knowledge, no new research into shared housing has emerged from social psychologists. Given the lack of attention to the topic by psychologists, there is plenty of scope for further research. While the positives of flatting are mentioned by our participants, these could be further investigated. The negative psychological implications of dysfunctional flatting have also not been adequately addressed. Researchers have raised the issue of inclusion inevitably raising the question of exclusion.[19] There are some hints about exclusion and bullying in our data but not sufficient to warrant in-depth discussion. One of the limitations of our work is that it relies on self-report, and as such participants seldom admit to responsibility for initiating tension. Bullying and exclusion is one avenue that needs to be explored if we are to gain more understanding of intragroup relationships in non-kin households. For example, how does it feel to be ostracised, used as a scapegoat for flat problems or asked to leave? Traumatic experiences may result in individuals seeking a more compassionate group to live with or alternative types of accommodation. A further shortcoming in our study is that by restricting interviews to those individuals currently house sharing, voices of those who have had such bad past experiences that they prefer not to flat, remain silent. These voices are more likely to provide detail on disadvantages and negative psychological aspects. Inclusion of those ill-disposed to flatting may also reveal a darker side to sharing, including "flatmates from hell".[20]

In this regard, Elinor Wilkinson and Ilana Ortega-Alcázar have researched the negative impact on the health and well-being of house sharing among young adults on welfare in Britain. With the steady deterioration and diminishing social housing stock many disadvantaged, vulnerable young people on insecure incomes live at the lowest end of the private rental housing market with strangers in poor-quality housing. Research on shared housing in South Korea found that when young adults are forced to live in shared housing the potential risk of social dysfunction of house sharers could increase, while a positive attitude towards shared housing was more likely to result in improved mental health. In Australia, Zahra Nasreen and Kristian Ruming have examined shared room housing, which differs from shared housing as sharing of bedrooms or living rooms for sleeping arrangements with non-related tenants and strangers is involved. Informal tenancy agreements and sublets result in insecurity. Sharing, when occurring in these low-income contexts, can lead to unwanted housemates and fear for personal safety. Financially forced to live this way, few of the participants in these studies found it possible to regard their accommodation as home, secure or stable.[21] Kim McKee, Adriana Soaita and Jennifer Hoolachan have investigated young sharers with less resources and less positive outcomes due to persisting intergenerational differences in income and family wealth.[22]

In contrast, our participants are not on the margins of society but older participants speak of a time when flatting begins to lose its appeal. Future studies could examine aspects of how and why this develops and to what extent this is determined by cultural rejection of sharing as an acceptable lifestyle for older adults. Some participants mention aspirations for home ownership and traditional coupledom in the long run, but these may not be the prime motivating factors for finally eschewing flatting.

How does shared living impact later domestic arrangements? Single participants who experienced living on their own found the existence lonely and returned to flatting. Would this be true of couples used to having others around, especially if partners' work hours do not coincide?

Traditionally the bulk of housework has been the culturally sanctioned role for women. In Australia, Kirsten Natalier[23] noted that male privilege of avoiding mundane housework remains entrenched, even in shared housing, but has exposure to non-genderised, egalitarian expectations of household chores contributed to a decline in these mores in coupledom and to what extent? In this New Zealand study, participants did note that some males were adept at shirking responsibilities but this was often accompanied by observations that other male flatmates are zealous housecleaners.

Sue Heath et al. conclude that the normality of culturally sanctioned conventional domestic practices should be questioned without discrediting or devaluing them. House sharing offers insight into how ideologies are being altered at both market and relational levels. Whereas young adults may regard shared flatting as a transitional means to an end, living arrangements and relationships that exist outside of kin and family should be further researched and valued: liminal households should not be regarded as lesser homes.[24]

Peter Mackie advocates for greater awareness of the political, economic and cultural forces that restrict young people's transitions to independent living.[25] These need to be better understood if government policies and housing provisions are to offer youth a choice that is not reliant on normative assumptions of households.[26] Policy makers need to be on the cutting edge of change. The suitability and availability of housing for young people need to be improved, particularly in the private rented sector with provisions made for shared housing. The negative effect of the physical building intended for nuclear families on interpersonal relationships, noted by Frances Baum as early as 1986,[27] is evident in our study. Given the growing increase in alternative household composition, we endorse the call for radical new design solutions in new forms of dwelling to suitably accommodate non-traditional families.[28]

Conclusion

Clearly, young adults are making the best of a lifestyle motivated primarily by economic challenges. As home ownership becomes increasingly unattainable, young adults are finding new ways of understanding and making home. Our study suggests that individuals are typically content and happy within their shared homes. Flats are not merely regarded as a roof overhead but havens of sanctuary in which to unwind, while appreciating the support and ready-made company and social life available. By carefully navigating the hazards of shared domestic living, which has few traditional markers, young adults demonstrate an acute understanding of the domestic dynamics, which impact the quality of their lives.

Notes

1 Keith Tuffin, *Understanding Critical Social Psychology* (London: SAGE, 2005), 165.
2 Richard Ronald, Oana Druta and Maren Godzik, "Japan's Urban Singles: Negotiating Alternatives to Family Households and Standard Housing Pathways," *Urban Geography* 39, no. 7 (2018): 1018–1040.

3 Ayoung Woo, Gi-Hyoug Cho and Jeongseob Kim, "Would You Share Your Home? The Multifaceted Determinants of Preference for Shared Housing Among Young Adults," *Applied Geography* 103 (2019): 12–21.
4 Oana Druta, Richard Ronald and Sue Heath, "Urban Singles and Shared Housing," *Social & Cultural Geography* 22, no. 9 (2021): 1195–1203.
5 For example: Zahra Nasreen and Kristian J. Ruming, "Shared Room Housing and Home: Unpacking the Home-Making Practices of Shared Room Tenants in Sydney, Australia," *Housing, Theory and Society* 38, no. 2 (2021): 152–172; Druta, Ronald and Heath, "Urban Singles"; Kim McKee, Adriana Mihaela Soaita and Jennifer Hoolachan, "'Generation Rent' and the Emotions of Private Renting: Self-Worth, Status and Insecurity Amongst Low-Income Renters," *Housing Studies* 35, no. 8 (2020): 1468–1487; Sophia Maalsen and Nicole Gurran, "Finding Home Online? The Digitalization of Share Housing and the Making of Home Through Absence," *Housing, Theory and Society* 39 (2021): 401–419, www.tandfonline.com/doi/abs/10.1080/14036096.2021.1986423?journalCode=shou20.
6 Maalsen and Gurran, "Finding Home Online."
7 Eric Klinenberg, *Going Solo: The Extraordinary Rise and Surprising Appeal of Living Alone* (New York: Penguin, 2012).
8 Julianne Holt-Lunstad, Timothy B. Smith, Mark Baker and David Stephenson, "Loneliness and Social Isolation as Risk Factors for Mortality: A Meta-Analytic Review," *Perspectives on Psychological Science* 10, no. 2 (2015): 227–237.
9 Vivek Murthy, *Together: The Healing Power of Human Connection in a Sometimes Lonely World* (New York: Harper Wave, 2020).
10 Christopher M. Masi, Hsi-Yuan Chen, Louise C. Hawkley and John T. Cacioppo, "A Meta-Analysis of Interventions to Reduce Loneliness," *Personality and Social Psychology Review* 15, no. 3 (2011): 219–266.
11 Frances Baum, "Shared Housing: Making Alternative Lifestyles Work," *Australian Journal of Social Issues* 24 (1986): 197–212; Sherry Ahrentzen, Double Indemnity or Double Delight? The Health Consequences of Shared Housing and "Doubling Up," *Journal of Social Issues* 59, no. 3 (2003): 547–568; Sue Heath and Elizabeth Cleaver, *Young, Free and Single? Twenty-Somethings and Household Change* (Hampshire: Palgrave Macmillan, 2003); Timothy D. May, "Shared Housing: The Sharing Economy Gives Roommates a New Image," *Christian Science Monitor*, March 30, 2014, https://www.csmonitor.com/The-Culture/Family/2014/0330/Shared-housing-The-sharing-economy-gives-roommates-a-new-image.
12 Peter Kemp and Julie Rugg, *The Single Room Rent: Its Impact on Young People* (York: University of York, Centre for Housing Policy, 1998).
13 Baum, "Shared Housing."
14 Hazel Christie, Moira Munro and Heidi Rettig, "Accommodating Students," *Journal of Youth Studies* 5 (2002): 209–235.
15 Matthew Easterbrook and Vivian L. Vignoles, "What Does It Mean to Belong? Interpersonal Bonds and Intragroup Similarities as Predictors of Felt Belonging in Different Types of Groups," *European Journal of Social Psychology* 43, no. 6 (2013): 455–462.
16 David B. Barker, "The Behavioral Analysis of Interpersonal Intimacy in Group Development," *Small Group Research* 22 (1991): 76–91.
17 Jeffrey J. Arnett, "Emerging Adulthood: Understanding the New Way of Coming of Age," *Emerging Adults in America: Coming of Age in the 21st Century* 22 (2006): 3–19.
18 Heath and Cleaver, *Young, Free and Single*.
19 Fred P. Bossellman, "Replaying the Tragedy of the Commons," *Yale Journal of Regulation* 13 (1996): 391–402; Heath and Cleaver, *Young, Free and Single*; Meagan E. Gallagher, Giorgio A. Tasca, Kerri Ritchie, Louise Balfour, Hilary Maxwell and Hany Bissada, "Interpersonal Learning Is Associated with Improved Self-Esteem in Group Psychotherapy for Women with Binge Eating Disorder," *Psychotherapy* 51 (2015): 66–77.
20 John Birmingham, *He Died With a Falafel in His Hand* (Sydney: Duffy & Snellgrove, 2001).

21 Elinor Wilkinson and Ilana Ortega-Alcázar, "Stranger Danger? The Intersectional Impacts of Shared Housing on Young People's Health & Wellbeing," *Health & Place* 60 (2019): 102–191; Jihun Oh and Jeongseob Kim, "Relationship between Mental Health and House Sharing: Evidence from Seoul," *International Journal of Environmental Research and Public Health* 18, no. 5 (2021): 2495. Nasreen and Ruming, "Shared Room Housing."

22 McKee, Soaita and Hoolachan, "Generation Rent."

23 Kristen Natalier, ""I'm Not His Wife": Doing Gender in Share Households," Unpublished Doctoral Thesis. University of Queensland, 2003.

24 Sue Heath, Katherine Davies, Gemma Edwards and Rachel M. Scicluna, *Shared Housing, Shared Lives: Everyday Experiences across the Lifecourse* (London: Routledge, 2019).

25 Peter MacKie, "Young People and Housing: Identifying the Key Issues," *International Journal of Housing Policy* 16, no. 2 (2016): 137–143.

26 Gill Jones, "Experimenting With Households and Inventing Homes, "*International Social Science Journal* 164 (2000): 183–194.

27 Baum, "Shared Housing."

28 Jones, "Experimenting With Households"; Andrew Beer and Debbie Faulkner, *Housing Transitions Through the Life Course: Aspirations, Needs and Policy* (Bristol: Policy Press, 2011); Eleanor Wilkinson, "Single People's Geographies of Home: Intimacy and Friendship Beyond 'The Family,'" *Environment and Planning* A 46, no. 10 (2014): 2452–2468.

INDEX